NORMAN VINCENT PEALE

by Richard Lewis Detrich

The Man, His Ministry

Foreword by Ruth Peale

Contents

ISBN 0-89542-068-6 595

Published by Ideals Publishing Corporation

11315 Watertown Plank Road

Milwaukee, Wis. 53226

Editorial Director, James Kuse

Managing Editor, Ralph Luedtke

Production Editor/Manager, Richard Lawson

Photographic Editor, Gerald Koser

Copy Editor, Sharon Style

Designed by Beverly Rae Wiersum

ACKNOWLEDGMENTS

Excerpts from the book THE ADVENTURE OF BEING A WIFE by Mrs. Norman Vincent Peale. © 1971 by Ruth S. Peale and Arthur Gordon. Published by Prentice-Hall, Inc., Englewood Cliffs, New Jersey 07632. Excerpts from the book ENTHU-SIASM MAKES THE DIFFERENCE by Norman Vincent Peale. © 1967 by Norman Vincent Peale. Published by Prentice-Hall, Inc., Englewood Cliffs, New Jersey 07632. Excerpts from the book ONE MAN'S WAY by Arthur Gordon. © 1972 by Norman Vincent Peale and Arthur Gordon. Published by Prentice-Hall, Inc., Englewood Cliffs, New Jersey 07632. Excerpts from the book POSITIVE THINKING FOR A TIME LIKE THIS by Norman Vincent Peale. © 1975 by Prentice-Hall, Inc. Published by Prentice-Hall, Inc., Englewood Cliffs, New Jersey 07632. Excerpts from the book THE POWER OF POSITIVE THINKING by Norman Vincent Peale. © 1952 by Prentice-Hall, Inc. Published by Prentice-Hall, Inc., Englewood Cliffs, New Jersey 07632. Excerpts from the book YOU CAN IF YOU THINK YOU CAN by Norman Vincent Peale. © 1974 by Norman Vincent Peale. Published by Prentice-Hall, Inc., Englewood Cliffs, New Jersey 07632. Excerpt: "I knew I was in a university pulpit . . ." from "God's Help Is Available To You" in THE CHRISTIAN HERALD, February, 1956. Excerpts: "At that moment . . ."; "It was the custom . . ."; "I began to work in this field . . ." from "Why I Preach As I Do" in THE CHRISTIAN HERALD, January, 1956. Reprinted with their permission. Excerpts from SIN, SEX AND SELF-CONTROL, by Norman Vincent Peale. Copyright © 1965 by Norman Vincent Peale. Reprinted by permission of Doubleday & Company, Inc. Excerpt: "I believe that the principles of Jesus Christ . . ." From THE NEW ART OF LIVING by Norman Vincent Peale. Copyright © 1937, 1971 by Norman Vincent Peale. Used by permission of Hawthorn Books, Inc. The following excerpts used with permission of Foundation For Christian Living: "I am the resurrection, and the life . . ."; "I shall never forget the second funeral . . ."; "Before you came into this world . . ." taken from LET NOT YOUR HEART BE TROUBLED, Copyright © 1966 by Norman Vincent Peale. "And you will be criticized . . ." from WHAT TO DO WHEN, Copyright © 1966 by Norman Vincent Peale. "It was a Sunday that Norman and I will never forget . . ."; "The sun was bombarding its eastern face . . ." from FAVORITE STORIES OF POSITIVE FAITH, Copyright © 1974 by Norman Vincent Peale.

If you would like to receive Creative Help for Daily Living, or a free copy of the booklet Let Not Your Heart Be Troubled write to: FCL, Box W-10, Pawling, N.Y. 12564.

PHOTO CREDITS

THE CHURCH HERALD, 3; GUIDEPOSTS, 1, 60, 64, 65, 74; Horatio Alger Awards Committee, 16, 20; LIFE MAGAZINE (Walter Sanders), 40; Marble Collegiate Church, 6, 15, 18, 26, 32, 44, 48, 55, 76, 79, 80; © Helen Marcus, 4, 22, 59, 63, 66, 70; Religious News Service, 29, 56; SUCCESS UNLIMITED MAGAZINE, 52, 73; "There's an Answer," 78; University United Methodist Church, 36, 37; Geri Vartanian, 9, 47, 50.

Foreword

This unique book by Richard Lewis Detrich captures the personality and narrates the story of Dr. Peale's ministry in a most interesting manner.

Norman and I, from our earliest days together, have been a dedicated team, you might say, working as best we can to advance the kingdom of our Lord and Savior Jesus Christ. The basic purpose of Dr. Peale's ministry, covering a period of almost fifty years at Marble Collegiate Church, and our work together, has been an emphasis upon changed lives through faith in Christ.

When I told Norman that I was writing this foreword he said, "Make it clear that we have always been a team and that you handle the organizational part of our ministry and I just do the talking."

The secret of Norman's preaching is: love of Christ, love of people, sincerity, and the use of everyday language and thought forms understandable by everyone, young and old. These factors have brought non-churchgoing people by the thousands under the influence of his ministry.

It has been my part of the teamwork to organize two aspects of Norman's ministry, the Foundation for Christian Living and *Guideposts* Magazine, and to direct these two large spiritual publishing enterprises.

Both of us thank our good friend, Richard Detrich, for his beautiful book. We admire him very much and have always had great interest in his creative ministry.

RUTH STAFFORD PEALE

Special Thanks

In sincere appreciation, I would like to thank the following people for their contributions toward the creation of this book:

Dr. Peale, for his friendship, encouragement, and permission to tell his story, and who, together with Mrs. Peale, provided helpful comments and assured the accuracy of this book.

Arthur Gordon, author of *Minister to Millions* and Editorial Director of *Guideposts*, for his valuable assistance; Myron Boardman, Executive Director of the Foundation for Christian Living and former President of the trade division of Prentice-Hall, who read the manuscript and offered excellent advice; Dr. Arthur Caliandro, the staff, and members of Marble Collegiate Church; Van Varner of *Guideposts*; and Dr. Peale's family and friends for allowing me to include their comments.

Barb De Young, who typed the manuscript; and Jim Kuse and Pat Pingry of Ideals, who stuck with me at times when the going was rough, and who helped a dream become a reality.

Peale and wife, Ruth, at their farm in Pawling, New York.

This Is Norman Vincent Peale

It's 10:30 P.M. I'm waiting in the mauve-colored lobby of the Pfister Hotel in downtown Milwaukee for Norman Vincent Peale. A few blocks away Dr. Peale is finishing up a speech to six thousand key sales people in Mecca Convention Center. It's basically the same speech he's delivered many times before, but the audience isn't aware of it. His timing is perfect! He leaves them rolling in the aisles with laughter and filled with a new sense of purpose and enthusiasm. Peale is perhaps at his best when speaking to a group of sales people: he understands them and they love him. He receives a standing ovation. He looks surprised and laughs somewhat self-deprecatingly as he acknowledges their applause and approval. Although it happens almost every time he speaks, each time he is surprised and pleased. Peale is very critical of himself. Regardless of the number of times he speaks, at the end of each speech he wonders if he did his best, or if he should have said something differently. He smiles, waves, and strides briskly off the platform into a waiting car.

A few minutes later he is walking through the lobby of the Pfister Hotel. It could have been a hotel anywhere: at least a fourth of Peale's life is lived in hotels. This week it might have been Tampa, Indianapolis, or St. Louis, but it's Thursday, so this must be Milwaukee. In an average week Peale speaks three or four times in cities scattered across the country, sometimes speaking in one city in the morning and in another, several thousand miles away, the same evening. Each year Peale logs over one hundred fifty thousand air miles. But this hotel lobby holds a special attraction for Peale. This is the original lobby of the Pfister Hotel, a rarity in days when buildings are crushed and discarded like empty soda cans. This lobby has been carefully preserved and restored to its original grandeur, the way it had been many years earlier when Dr. Charles Clifford Peale, M.D., Norman's father, had lived near the Pfister Hotel where he dined each night while working as a public health officer for the city of Milwaukee. Peale is nostalgic as he thinks of his own father striding through this very hotel lobby long before Charles Peale had ever met Norman's mother.

Milwaukee is known for its German heritage which has produced fine beer and delicious German food specialties. But Peale's convictions against any kind of strong drink are well known, so the committee selected a box of fine sausages to take home as a remembrance of his trip to Milwaukee. In Florida they gave him oranges and grapefruit. Last week in Washington state it was apples. Obviously it's impossible for him to lug along all the gifts he's presented by admirers and companies who want to plug their products, so many are mailed to him, some are shared with others, and a few are left behind, a fact which delights hotel chambermaids.

We visit upstairs in his hotel room and talk about his father's early days in Milwaukee and Norman recalls that his father used to reminisce about the Pfister Hotel and his office which was only a few blocks away. He makes a mental note to ask to drive by that area on his way to the airport. He asks about my family and wants to see pictures of my children.

As I'm ready to leave, Peale asks me to wait while he rummages in the hotel dresser and pulls out a clear plastic laundry bag. Since Norman Vincent Peale is a V.I.P. guest in any hotel, there is a huge basket of fruit and cheese in his room, compliments of the hotel manager. He scoops the fruit and cheese into the laundry bag and gives it to me to take home, noting that he knows how hard it is sometimes to make ends meet on a preacher's salary. I appreciate his thoughtfulness, but can't help but wonder if he really does remember those days back when he was a young, unknown preacher, just starting out and trying to make ends meet. I almost get the sausages, too, but since the man who made the presentation is driving him to the airport, and since he's headed back to New York, Dr. Peale decides to keep the wieners.

Peale delivers a Sunday morning sermon in Marble Collegiate Church.

He asks to borrow my black, felt-tipped pen and writes boldly across the white Usinger's carton in big, firm, enthusiastic letters, "NORMAN VINCENT PEALE, 1025 Fifth Avenue, New York." He puts the pen down, steps back, admires his handiwork and proclaims, "There! Now I *dare* anyone to steal that!"

It's hard to imagine that Norman Vincent Peale could have been Tom, Dick, or Harry Peale. Worse yet, if someone hadn't come up with a name, he could have just been "baby boy Peale." The Peales were so proud of their firstborn son that they almost didn't come up with a name for him. When his aunt arrived on the scene the baby still didn't have a name. She took charge, reportedly challenging her brother, "Charles, if you don't name this baby, I will!" And she did! She had a favorite line from a Tennyson poem which inspired the name. It went, "Kind hearts are more than coronets, and simple faith than Norman blood." So she suggested "Norman" and Norman it was. Practical, ecclesio-political considerations helped contribute the middle name. Norman's father, a medical doctor turned Methodist minister, named his son after his ecclesiastical superior, Bishop Vincent.

His parents and Aunt Mae may have been well-satisfied with that stirring name, but Peale wasn't, at least not always. As a schoolboy, with visions of someday entering politics, he decided "Norman Vincent Peale" just didn't have the proper presidential-ring to it, and so he changed his name and began signing it "William Howard Peale." He had visions of his image cast in bronze standing outside the capitol of Ohio. He went so far as to inquire at the courthouse how he might make the change legal. But the political ambitions were soon forgotten, as was the new name. Norman Vincent Peale it was, and is.

Peale was born in 1898. Now in his eighties, he keeps a schedule that would leave most younger men exhausted! Few people, certainly not the members of his church or even close associates, can fully comprehend the vastness of Peale's outreach and ministry and the demands placed on him. Everyone wants "just a minute" of Peale's time and when you are "minister to millions" there just aren't enough minutes to go around. The Peales work constantly and are always on the go. Peale's long-time personal secretary Mary Creighton says, "I hardly ever see him! We communicate mostly by memo." But Peale and his wife seem to flourish under the pressure.

To understand Peale you have to understand what he calls his "jobs." His oldest job, and the one that means the most to him, is as minister of Marble Collegiate Church. The Collegiate Church was begun in 1628 shortly after the Dutch settled the island which was bought from the Manhatoe Indians and is not just one church, but a collective of several worshiping congregations in which all the ministers are colleagues. All of these churches share a common Consistory, or board of directors, and pool their resources. Although Peale came to pastor Marble Collegiate Church in 1932, it was not until 1973 that he actually became the Senior Minister of the Collegiate Church. The same year Peale began at Marble, Dr. Ernest Palen came to Middle Collegiate Church. Palen was installed a few weeks before Peale and so Dr. Palen became Senior Minister of the Collegiate Church and continued in that position until his death in 1973. It was not until then that Dr. Peale actually became the Senior Minister of the Collegiate Church.

Peale is still actively involved in the life and ministry of Marble Collegiate Church. Except during the summer months and January, Peale preaches each Sunday at the 11:15 A.M. service at Marble. The actual administration of the day to day operation of the church has for many years been controlled more by the spirit of Norman Peale than by his person and presence. He has had to rely on carefully selected and trusted associates to run the operation of the church and meet the pastoral needs of the Marble congregation. Today Marble Collegiate Church is really run by Dr. Arthur Caliandro. Caliandro, like Peale, is a former Methodist clergyman who transferred to the Reformed Church In America when he came to Marble in 1962. Peale says, "At the church I have people like Art who do things that I as the Senior Pastor should be doing. He is a pastor and a businessman and runs the church." Caliandro is Peale's heir apparent at Marble and has been carefully groomed for the job. But Peale has no intentions of retiring. "My basic job," he says, "because I've had it so long and it means more to me than anything else, is preaching in the church! I've never considered retiring from the church!" But the church is only one of Peale's many "jobs."

Peale and his wife are co-publishers of *Guideposts* magazine and are actively involved in the

Although dwarfed by the nearby Empire State Building, Marble Collegiate Church occupies a prominent place on the corner of West 29th Street and 5th Avenue.

management of *Guideposts*. "Together we run the business of *Guideposts*," says Peale. "I'm president, Ruth's executive vice-president. She and I are co-publishers. Whenever we have a board meeting, or an operating meeting, we're both there. We employ about five hundred people at *Guideposts*. We've employed people who are knowledgeable professionals and we've got a staff of the finest and best trained people you can find." That's another job.

The "speaking business" is another major Peale endeavor. Two or three days every week frequently accompanied by Ruth, Peale is out criss-crossing the country speaking to packed houses at conventions and sales meetings. He cannot possibly accept all the invitations and opportunities to speak which are extended to him and must decline several for each one accepted.

The Foundation for Christian Living is another Peale enterprise, this one begun and headed by Ruth Peale. The Foundation is headquartered today in a comfortable, pleasant building at Pawling, New York, and employs one hundred and twenty-five people who handle Peale's correspondence and distribute advice, sermons, and booklets by Dr. Peale. This headquarters is considered one of the finest direct mail operations in the country. All this began rather humbly on the kitchen table of the Peale home where Ruth and a handful of volunteers would mail out printed copies of Peale's early sermons. Today a monthly selection of Peale sermons is mailed out to upward of three quarters of a million members of the "FCL family." "FCL" is a nonprofit foundation which distributes Peale literature free of charge, but hopefully for a donation to cover the costs of printing. Over one and a half million copies of a recent booklet on healing have been distributed through the Foundation. The Foundation for Christian Living is probably the largest religious literature distributing organization in the world.

Another Peale "job" is his weekly, syndicated newspaper column *There's an Answer!* which appears in seven hundred newspapers across the country with a total readership of twenty-seven million people!

A more recent Peale "job" is "The American Character," a nationally syndicated radio program broadcast three hundred times a day on a hundred and eighty-five radio stations across the country. "The American Character" is funded by ITT and aims at counterbalancing the media emphasis on what is wrong with our society through daily ninety second reports about what is right with Americans. Each broadcast, narrated by Dr. Peale, focuses on a vignette of modern day American goodness and courage.

There are other Peale jobs. Peale's messages are taped on television and are syndicated across the country. Cassette tapes of his sermons are distributed by the Foundation for Christian Living. He and Ruth serve on many boards of directors. Until recently Peale was chairman of the Horatio Alger Awards Committee. He serves on the board of Central College in Pella, Iowa, and Ruth is on the Board of Hope College, Holland, Michigan, both schools of the Reformed Church in America.

Probably Peale's best-known "job" is as a writer. He's written twenty-one books and co-authored two others. His best-known work *The Power of Positive Thinking* has sold over ten million copies in thirty three languages.

To keep this vast ministry going requires the constant attention of Dr. and Mrs. Peale. They work all the time, even when they travel. "We've got all these masses of paper along and we're working constantly," says Norman. "If you were to go along on the train with us from New York to Carmel, where we're going to *Guideposts* it would be pretty much business all the way up and back. 'What do you think about the performance of this guy?' Or, 'What about this one, that one? What do you think we ought to do about this?'

"We don't accept social engagements either on the road or here, or anywhere. We haven't got the time! When we're not working we try to rest. But even then . . . we work all the time! All the time. We've got to in order to handle all these responsibilities. It's the kind of life I wouldn't recommend to anyone!"

Peale denies being a workaholic. He says, "I'm not a workaholic in that work doesn't control me. And it doesn't control Ruth. We work. We like to do it or we wouldn't do it. We enjoy working. In order to handle the seven or eight different jobs we have, or things we control, we have to constantly keep at it."

Ruth Peale says, "If there isn't a book under contract, there are always newspaper columns or magazine articles to write, manuscripts to edit, sermons to be outlined, people to see. Norman hates to be idle; a friend of his once said that he has a 'lust for work.' He's really incapable of sustained loafing. Unless he feels that he is accomplishing something, he's miserable.

"I must confess, that to a degree, I'm the same way. So we get a lot of work done. But we also try to find time for recreation in the literal sense of the word. We love to read. (Norman can easily read a book a day, which frustrates me because I'm so much slower.) We go to the opera and concerts; we mingle among the people wherever we are . . . We try to find periods of quietness, of withdrawal, of inspiration where the batteries can be recharged.

"This is not something you can command; you can't leap up in the morning and announce, 'Today we are going to get our creativity restored.' It's a more subtle thing. We try not to be regimented or harrassed by schedules so that we can take a quiet walk or expose ourselves to the majesty of the mountains or the vastness of the sea. Or watch a sun rise or tramp a country road in the rain. In other words, we aim to make ourselves as receptive as possible to the life forces that surround and sustain us all."

But you get the definite impression from talking to Peale that these interludes in life have become rarer and rarer. Sometimes, however, it gets ridiculous and Peale rebels. In one city he was met and rushed from one bookstore autograph session to another, rushed to a luncheon where he spoke, then rushed to an author's reception. He was rushed back to his hotel, rushed to dress for dinner, and in the midst of all this rushing the telephone rang and he was told to hurry and get down for dinner. Enough was enough! All of a sudden Peale asked himself, "Why am I rushing? What's the meaning of this ceaseless rush?"

Deliberately he took off his coat, loosened his tie, kicked off his shoes, wiggled his toes in the carpet, sat down and propped his feet up on the bed. He picked up his Bible and opened it to Psalm 121 and read these magnificent words: "I will lift up my eyes to the hills. From whence does my help come? My help comes from the Lord, who made heaven and earth." He sat there in prayer, meditating on those words while the world rushed on without him for a while. It became an "amazing experience of the healing power of God." Fifteen minutes later he went down to dinner. The world had survived without him. He had missed only the soup which he

later discovered was "by general consent no great loss."

More recently the Peales were in Holland hosting a 350th anniversary tour to the birthplace of the Collegiate Church. Each year Norman and Ruth travel all over the country, working all the time. But enough is enough. In Holland Peale told his wife, "Look, let's you and I just drop all work for the next four days."

The Peales were traveling with a group of over a hundred people. "Normally we wouldn't take bus trips," says Peale. "I see people all over the world in tourist buses and I've always said you'd never get me in one. We've been to Holland several times and we've been to all the places the buses were going. But I said to Ruth, 'Let's get in these buses and take these tours!' She said, 'I'm astonished to hear you say that!' But we did it and to our great surprise we enjoyed it! But that's the exception."

The Peales' work requires a great deal of travel, but if there is any hobby that they have, it's probably also travel. Ruth says, "Perhaps the greatest benefit in travel is the stimulus of novelty. As you move about, you meet new people, you encounter new ideas, observe new customs, hear new stories. For Norman and me, these experiences are not only stimulating in themselves, they supply the raw material that Norman draws on for radio talks and sermons, lectures and newspaper columns all through the winter months. Many people, I'm sure, think of a writer as someone who, like a kind of human spider, spins his webs out of a magical and inexhaustible reservoir inside him. But this isn't so. You have to take in something before you can send it back out. The creative process that receives this 'something' reshapes it, gives it form and substance and drama. But there has to be a steady input, or the well will run dry."

Traveling with Ruth Peale must be a joy, for she attends to all the checking in and checking out of hotels. Since the Peales are on the road a quarter of their time, Ruth Peale tries hard to make each new hotel room as comfortable and homey as possible. At each stop she completely unpacks and places everything into the dresser drawers, hiding the suitcases out of sight. She carries with her pictures of the family which she props up around the hotel room, and places books and magazines on end tables, so that in five minutes the room looks like they've always lived there.

The Power of the Positive Peale

It's a cold, wet, October night in New York City. Lights of bumper to bumper traffic reflect off wet pavement on the East Side Drive, also known as the FDR Drive. The couple in the Mercedes sports coupe have never been fans of the "New Deal" and prefer "East Side Drive." Their car, license plate "RSP," exits the FDR and heads over the Willis Avenue bridge into a strange and different world—the South Bronx.

Norman and Ruth Peale are a long way from Fifth Avenue! This is a different New York—not the New York tourists visit, nor the New York that's the hub of commerce and communication, but the real New York. This is it. This, and Bedford-Stuyvesant, Highbridge, and East Harlem. This is the real New York, where it's all happening, the good and the bad. This is the core of the Big Apple.

The car is easy to spot as it pulls off the Willis Avenue bridge. An unmarked police car pulls out and tails the Mercedes up Willis Avenue. Kids hanging out on the street corner spot the Mercedes stopped for the light. Basketball star Nate Archibald who grew up in this housing project, drives a similar car. A quick glance at the occupants confirms it's not "Tiny" Archibald.

There are four white people on Willis Avenue, two in the Mercedes and two in the police car. This is 1968. Not a good year in the South Bronx for whites or cops. Or blacks. It's not a good year for anyone. New York is the only city in the nation that hasn't erupted in a major urban convulsion. It appears cool on the surface but underneath it's boiling. Kids are armed and training for revolution. Everyone is nervous. This is the year they're killing cops in the Bronx.

The cars turn onto East 146th Street and Ruth Peale pulls into a parking space in front of an old, run-down ghetto church. The unmarked patrol car drives slowly by. An illuminated white cross with half the bulbs burned out hangs over the sidewalk. The Peales get out and enter the church. Four teenagers immediately surround the car with only one mission: keep all the tires on the Peale's car. The South Bronx is that kind of place.

This is the night of my ordination and installation to the ministry. When I first faced the challenge of pastoring the Mott Haven Reformed Church in the heart of the South Bronx, I knew we faced tremendous obstacles. If this church was going to do anything we needed three things: help, help, and help. Four things. We also needed money. Since Norman Vincent Peale was pastor of the largest and most heavily endowed Reformed Church in the country I thought if anyone could help us he could. And he later did. But first he needed to see this little church and feel its possibilities. I inquired if he ever attended this kind of function and was told, "Yes, I've preached in a Black church in Harlem and helped start a very successful counseling service on 125th Street, in the heart of the ghetto. As president of NYC Council of Churches, I was available to any pastor who wanted me." I knew how busy he was and felt certain that it would be impossible for him to come, but I asked him anyway, and he accepted. I didn't ask him to preach—that honor belonged to my father—I asked him to give the "challenge to the minister," the minister being me.

I was eager with anticipation as I walked into the room where the reverend members of the Classis of New York were robing. This was my chance to meet the great Dr. Norman Vincent Peale in person. When I walked in Dr. Peale had his robe half on— and the zipper was stuck. Mrs. Peale was stooped over trying to get the zipper unstuck. What a revelation! I don't know what I expected, but I never thought Norman Vincent Peale's zippers ever got stuck! He wasn't ten feet tall either—more like five foot nine inches. His feet touched the same ground as mine. He was warm, friendly, unassuming and for a moment I had the impression that my own grandfather had come down for my ordination.

What I didn't know when I asked Peale to share in my ordination was that thirty-six years earlier, to the day, Dr. Peale had been installed as minister of Marble Collegiate Church and his father had preached the sermon. I vividly remember the words with which Dr. Peale launched me into the ministry. He said, "I can assure you that for many years you

Mott Haven Reformed Church in the Bronx, where Peale spoke at the author's ordination.

will remember this evening and there will come a day in the long future when it will mean even more to you than it does tonight. As I heard your father preaching a good, solid, steadfast exposition of the gospel, my mind went back thirty-six years ago tonight when I heard my own father under similar circumstances speak to me. He said, 'Norman, I believe in you. Never fail me and my teachings, but above all never fail Christ.' My father is now gone from this world, but the admonition he gave me then was fresh in my mind tonight.

"It's very highly presumptuous of me to give any advice to a young minister. I have a hard enough time dealing with myself! One basic thing: preach Christ! He's the only asset we have, Christ crucified, the Lord and Savior, Christ the divine Son of God, Christ our elder brother.

"Another thing is this: remember that you have a job to reconstruct society and this is a tough one. This society today is increasingly evil and pagan, unjust, inequities exist among us, and this society has got to be changed. Who is going to change it—somebody who will destroy it, or somebody who will help create it? I myself think the minister is an agent of social reconstruction, but it must always be in the name of Christ.

"I would also suggest that every time you walk through this community you rejoice that you are located here. For this community is full to overflowing with opportunity! Love the people. You love them and let them know that you love them, and they'll love you and you'll lead them to Christ and your ministry will be rich and full."

I'll never forget that evening! I began to realize that problems are opportunities. Probably more than any other evening of my life it helped me determine the direction I wanted to go and the type of ministry I wanted to develop. Norman Vincent Peale didn't have to take the time to come up to the South Bronx to a little church nobody had ever heard of and challenge a young man just out of seminary. But he did! And over the years that I've known him he's seized opportunities to encourage me in my ministry.

Peale is an enormously powerful man. He would deny it, but it's true. *The Power of Positive Thinking* alone has sold over ten million copies. Multiply that by three or four and you'll have the number of people all over the world who have been inspired and helped by that one book! *Guideposts* magazine is the fifteenth largest magazine in the country with a readership which probably exceeds twelve million people! Peale directly employs over seven hundred people in his various ministries.

It's another rainy day. This is Sunday morning and—most unusually—the Peales are not at Marble Collegiate Church. They are sharing a late continental breakfast of coffee and Danish with longtime friends. They chat in the brightly decorated gold and yellow sitting room of their friends' home. The bright decor contrasts with the gloomy world outside. The house happens to be the White House and their old friend, the President of the United States.

After breakfast and small talk they leave the Presidential family's private sitting room and go downstairs to the magnificent East Room. The Nixons and the Peales enter the East Room, smiling. The two hundred or so people already gathered for the nondenominational service stand as the President enters the room. After the invocation, a hymn, and a selection by a Black choir, the President introduces his old friend, Norman Vincent Peale.

Peale rises and stands at a solitary microphone, under the huge crystal chandeliers of the East Room and delivers a warm, folksy message, not unlike the message he would be giving if he were back in New York at Marble Church. The service lasts only half an hour and afterwards there is a reception with the preacher and the President greeting all present.

Later the Nixons will escort Dr. and Mrs. Peale to the family floor where, after a personally conducted tour of the Presidential living quarters, the two families will lunch in the President's private dining room. After lunch they will retire to a sitting room where the President will ask Norman Vincent Peale to represent him as a special envoy to visit and inspire our troops in Vietnam.

Peale's relationship with former President Nixon goes back over many years. Peale has been a friend and pastor to the Nixons and their family for years. During World War II New York was crowded with service men and women. Marble Collegiate Church seized this opportunity and created a variety of ministries to service people. Peale recalls that during those days, "You'd look at the congregation and it would be fifty percent uniforms." He says, "Everywhere I go, even today which is over thirty years later, I meet people who were here then. They'll say to me that what they found here really saved their lives, saved their sanity, and gave them new hope. Some of these people became real leaders in their various lines of work." This is how Peale

Peale speaks to packed halls at conventions and sales meetings all over the country, averaging three speeches per week.

Former President Herbert Hoover receives the Horatio Alger Award from Peale and Kenneth J. Beebe, founder of the Awards.

first met Richard Nixon. "He was down at 30 Church Street in Naval Headquarters and he used to come up here to church every Sunday with his wife. Then later I got to know the kids."

Regardless of Richard Nixon's later short-comings, or for that matter our own, Nixon was President of the United States. Peale explains why he's remained mum about Richard Nixon. "I've always had a very strong feeling for the sacredness of the pastoral relationship. Reporter after reporter has tried to get me to say something about him and I tell them, 'Mr. Nixon was my parishioner and my friend and my relationship with him is sacred business. I wouldn't talk about him more than I would any other parishioner.' We stayed overnight with them several times in the White House and I

knew him very well. I've had other parishioners who did things that people criticized, but he just happened to be more prominent." Peale points out that there is a danger in taking so much delight in another person's problems, or in the collapse of a man's character or reputation, that you become the greater sinner in the process.

The fact is that Peale had been to the White House many times before Richard Nixon became President. Peale is no stranger to the Oval Office. He has been associated with and known several presidents including Herbert Hoover, Harry Truman, and Dwight Eisenhower.

Around the world the Peales have been received by all manner of royalty, presidents, ambassadors, and the princes of commerce and industry. When traveling in the Phillipines the Peales were invited to a state dinner by President and Mrs. Marcos. Taiwan's Generalissimo and Madame Chiang Kai-shek invited them to spend several days at their summer residence.

And it's not just the royal and the famous. Everyone wants just a moment of Peale's time. People stop him in restaurants, hotel lobbies, airports, and even corner him in taxis and restrooms to tell him what a difference his books and ministry have made in their lives. He is an incredibly busy man but when you talk to him you don't feel it. When he talks to you, he talks to you. There may be fifty other people waiting in line to talk with him, he may be mulling over four or five projects, and he may have a thousand miles to travel before his day is done. But for that moment all of his attention is focused on you. You are important! Unbelievable as it may seem, in that moment Norman Vincent Peale is actually honored to know *you*. What proves it is that he remembers these encounters with people and retells them in his books in minute detail. He may change the names, but he remembers vividly the encounters.

Peale treats people as people, no matter who they are. He can drop the names of the rich and powerful without blushing or hesitation. "As Herbert Hoover once said to me . . ." Or, "I was talking with the Queen the other day . . ." Yet he can and does take three whole pages in *Enthusiasm Makes the Difference* to describe in detail a conversation he had with Hans, a busboy in a European hotel. He's just as serious about Hans as he is about the Queen. In Peale's eyes they are both equally important. Dr. Arthur Caliandro, his associate of fifteen years, says that Dr. Peale is the same wherever he is and whomever he is with. "In a board meeting, talking to a cab driver, sitting in his living room, he's the same man. More than one person has told me that Dr. Peale has yet to realize how big and important he really is. In Australia he was mobbed like a movie star, but it never turned his head. And one time when Dr. Peale went out to San Clemente, I am told, he stood outside the gate scratching his head, then asked a boy on a bike, 'Say, son, where's the doorbell to this place?'"

I asked him once, "How do you keep from being overly impressed with yourself? After all, you're the great Dr. Peale?"

Without a moment's hesitation he answered, "That's easy! I know myself! That's what keeps me from getting overly impressed." Then, after a long pause, he added, "I've lived with myself too long."

I protested, "But you're so down-to-earth! It's almost like you've tracked Ohio mud onto Fifth Avenue."

His face lit up. He grabbed a pen and paper and started scribbling and said, "That's a good phrase! 'Ohio mud on Fifth Avenue!' I like that!"

At one time I suspected all this humility must be a put on. Judging from the way some writers and reporters have written about Dr. Peale, they must think so too. He's hard to believe, but I'm convinced it's real. The man is genuine. He really is down-to-earth and not at all impressed with himself.

Peale says, "I've always been this way! It's my nature I guess. I know when I go around the country the reporters always refer to this kind of drawly, gravelly voice that I have and my down-to-earth Ohio talk. I don't try to be this way. It's just the way I am. I never liked pretentiousness or stuffiness."

I asked if he treated corporation heads, presidents, and heads of state with the same down-to-earth friendliness.

"Yes! Exactly! I met the Queen the other day in Holland . . . " He says it like she's Mary Smith or the lady in the apartment down the hall. He's talking about her Royal Majesty, Queen Julianna of the Netherlands.

"She's the same type of down-to-earth person. You go to the palace and you think it's going to be 'your majesty' and 'your royal highness' but there was none of that. She was just a nice, lovely, kind-hearted, middle-aged woman. We were told she is sixty-nine. No stuffiness. I just talked with her. I said, 'You might be interested to know I was on a Dutch ship in the Caribbean,' and I wasn't sure of the correct pronounciation. So I pronounced it one way, and then I said, 'or is it the Caribbean,' pronouncing it the other way. She said, 'You got me! Either way is all right!'

"I said, 'Well whichever it is, I was on the old SS *STATENDAM* the night Princess Beatrix was born, and the captain asked me to say a prayer for the new princess.' She looked at me and said, 'You know something? You and I have been around for a long time!' She was down-to-earth! I liked her!"

Peale has ten rules as listed in his bestseller, *The Power of Positive Thinking*, that he's applied to his dealings with people through the years. He applies them without discrimination to princes and paupers alike.

1. Learn to remember names. Inefficiency at this point may indicate that your interest is not sufficiently outgoing. A man's name is very important to him.

2. Be a comfortable person so there is no strain in being with you—be an old-shoe, old-hat kind of individual. Be homey.

3. Acquire the quality of relaxed easy-goingness so that things do not ruffle you.

4. Don't be egotistical. Guard against giving the impression that you know it all. Be natural and normally humble.

5. Cultivate the quality of being interesting so that people will want to be with you and get something of stimulating value from their association with you.

6. Study to get the 'scratchy' elements out of your personality, even those of which you may be unconscious.

7. Sincerely attempt to heal, on an honest Christian basis, every misunderstanding you have had or now have. Drain off your grievances.

8. Practice liking people until you learn to do so genuinely. Remember what Will Rogers said, 'I never met a man I didn't like.' Try to be that way.

9. Never miss an opportunity to say a word of congratulation upon anyone's achievement, or express sympathy in sorrow or disappointment.

10. Get a deep spiritual experience so that you have something to give people that will help them to be stronger and meet life more effectively. Give strength to people and they will give affection to you.

Peale cares about people. His concern is real and genuine. Sometimes while he travels he engages in a practice of shooting prayers at the people he sees along the way. These are people he doesn't know and probably will never meet. But he realizes in a mystical and spiritual way that his life touches theirs for a fraction of an instant. As the train for Pawling burrows up from the underground tracks that run beneath midtown Manhattan and rises to an elevated track somewhere in Harlem, Peale looks out and sees a woman hanging a blanket out to air from the window of a tenement along the track. For a moment their lives touch and he shoots a prayer her way. He sees a little kid standing on a street corner below, full of potential and possibilities, and he shoots a prayer for that child's future in his direction.

Following his speech, Peale greets a member of the audience.

Peale confers with Harold A. Robinson, Vice-President of the National Conference of Christians and Jews, prior to accepting the Conference's Media Award for "The American Character."

Gregg Warhurst is a twelve-year-old member of Marble Collegiate Church who lives in suburban New Jersey. Gregg thinks Dr. Peale is the greatest, partly because his birthday falls on May 31st, the same as Peale's. When he was eight Gregg wrote a little letter to Peale observing that they shared the same birthday. That May 31st Dr. Peale called Gregg to the pulpit and invited him, following the service, into his office to share in Peale's birthday party. This has now become a yearly ritual for Dr. Peale and young Gregg Warhurst.

These are the little things about Peale which help make him the unusual man he is. And these are the little things which seldom get mentioned in articles and stories about Peale.

Peale's power rests not in his success, nor in his publishing dynasty, or even in his prestigious Fifth Avenue church, but in the fact that he truly loves people and cares about them. He is able to touch and inspire both saints and sinners. In his unpretentious, even folksy way, he can put his finger on the

need of the rich and famous, as well as ordinary folks like us.

The night of my ordination Peale told me, "I don't believe anybody can be a very good minister of Jesus Christ who hasn't got penetrating insight. You can't go to any college in the country and get a course in insight. There's no chair of insight at any university in the land. If you haven't got insight you can't get it by education, although it can be improved by education. Insight is the gift of God. It is the ability to look into the human heart and perceive what is actually there. It is an empathetic procedure in which you get inside a person and think from within out." He thought a while and added, "The other thing is love: love the people. You love them and let them know that you love them and they'll love you, and you'll lead them to Christ, and your ministry will be rich and full. Just love them." The secret of Norman Vincent Peale's power and success is his great insight into the human spirit and the great love that he has for people of all kinds.

19

Waldorf

The Successful Life

The lives of both Norman and Ruth Peale are Horatio Alger rags-to-riches stories. Peale received the Horatio Alger Award in 1952 and for many years served as chairman of the Award Committee. In 1977 he, as chairman, presented the Horatio Alger Award to his wife, Ruth. The award is presented to, "individuals, who, by their own efforts, have pulled themselves up by their bootstraps in the American tradition, have produced living proof that the free enterprise system of achieving success still offers equal opportunity to all."

Reporters like to comment on Peale's financial success though a minister. No one can deny that he is successful in many ways, including financially. It's impossible to sell over ten million copies of one book and not be financially successful; but what these writers fail to mention is that both Ruth and Norman Peale grew up in very poor ministers' families, or that they give far more than a tithe to worthwhile causes everywhere. Ruth's mother, after visiting with them in New York, said to her, one day, "Ruth, I have been observing your life. You don't really have more money than before, you just handle more." How true!

Norman Peale's father eventually became a Methodist District Superintendent, and although he never made more than $4,800 a year, the Peales lived in luxury compared to the Staffords. Ruth's father, also a minister, never earned more than $2,400 a year. Granted, dollars in those days bought more than dollars do today, but it was still a meager, sometimes hand-to-mouth existence in both families.

A particular traumatic, money-related event occurred in Ruth's life during World War I when a patriotic teacher asked all the children whose families had bought war bonds to stand up. Ruth was the only one who remained seated. Humiliated to tears, she ran home to ask her mother why they hadn't bought war bonds. There wasn't even enough money in the Stafford household to buy essentials, let alone finance the war. It was a humiliating experience that Ruth Stafford never forgot.

Peale's parents scrimped and saved to put him through Ohio Wesleyan University. He worked his own way through seminary running a dumb waiter at the Boston Y.M.C.A., and likes to call himself, 'the dumbest waiter the 'Y' ever had."

After high school Ruth went to City College in Detroit where tuition was free. At the same time her older brother Chuck was a senior at Syracuse University. Family finances were strained beyond the breaking point and it was necessary for Ruth to drop out of college and work in order to help her older brother complete his education. The agreement was that when Chuck completed his education he would then help Ruth with hers. So without any great enthusiasm, Ruth Stafford left City College to work for the Michigan Bell Telephone Company. She later observed that her decision was really providential, for had she gone ahead with college in Detroit she would never have met and married Norman Peale.

Peale has not forgotten what it was like to scrimp to make ends meet. Despite everything, he can be a frugal soul, sometimes setting out in a strange city on foot searching for a lunch counter rather than pay the exhorbitant prices for hotel room service. In spite of this thriftiness, and perhaps because of his own lean days, Dr. Peale once felt convicted because he did not tip as generously as he could afford and determined in the future to become a more generous tipper.

The Peales live on the East Side of New York at Eighty-fourth Street and Fifth Avenue, just across from Central Park and the Metropolitan Museum of Art. Three doors up the street is the permanent mission of the People's Republic of Bulgaria to the United Nations. Consulates and limousines abound in this fashionable area of New York. When they first came to the city in 1932, the Peales lived at Gramercy Park Hotel. When they were expecting their first child, they moved into an apartment at 25 Fifth Avenue. Later they moved up to 40 Fifth Avenue and finally to their current home overlooking Central Park. The three bedroom apartment is a parsonage, which means it is owned by the Marble Collegiate Church and provided for the Peales. Such an arrangement is typical in many churches where, in addition to salary, the church provides a parsonage or manse to the pastor.

The Peales have a home of their own in Pawling, a sleepy little village two hours drive, seventy-five miles north of the city. Pawling is an extraordinary little town, especially the twelve-mile ridge called "Quaker Hill" where the mailboxes have had such names as Edward R. Murrow, Lowell Thomas, Thomas Dewey, and, of course, Norman Vincent Peale. Not your typical, average neighborhood by any means! They were lured to Pawling in 1943 after they spent the summer at a home owned by his friend, Lowell Thomas. The Peales had been married for thirteen years and had never owned a home of their own. They'd always lived in apartments owned by the church. With the children growing up they wanted a place where the kids would see trees, grass, and hills.

Mrs. Peale describes how they bought the farm at Pawling. "I fell in love with the house at first sight. It was an old Eighteenth Century farmhouse set in about twenty acres of lovely, rolling countryside. It had a wide lawn with great stately maples. There were original hinges on some of the doors, wide hand-hewn floor boards, four fireplaces—with an old brick oven built into the largest one—and andirons that had supported blazing logs for more than a hundred and fifty years . . . oh, all sorts of marvelous things!

"I was dying to buy that house, but Norman said flatly, 'No' and gave all sorts of reasons. We didn't have the money (this was true, but I knew we could borrow it); the house was too big; we'd rattle around in it (this was not so true; three children and some pets can fill up almost any house). Finally, he said the neighbor's barn cut off the view (the barn did cut off some of the view, but not all—anyway it was a gem of a barn: antique, picturesque, an impressive part of the landscape).

"I tried to point out some of the features of the house that appealed to me, but Norman was not in the mood for listening. 'I'm sorry,' he said, 'We can't afford it, and I'm all against it, so you better forget about it.'

"I was tempted to argue, but I didn't. I didn't because I knew the frugality built into Norman during his childhood was a very real and powerful thing. He was appalled by the prospect of going heavily into debt. I knew that summoning up the determination to break through that childhood conditioning would take time—and that nothing I

Ruth and Norman spend a rare moment relaxing in the garden of their home in Pawling, New York.

could say could hurry the process. So I decided to wait until the timing was right.

"While I waited, though, I applied the second rule of persuasion: self-interest. I didn't specify what place, but I reminded Norman from time to time he needed a quiet, restful place to think, to write, to plan his speeches and sermons. I said I thought he would work better if he owned a piece of land somewhere. I remember I also got our friend Lowell Thomas, for whom Norman has great respect and affection, and who also lived at Pawling, to tell him that the barn, with its hand-hewn beams, was one of the finest in the whole state of New York! Which it is.

"I also worked on creating a climate of acqui-

escence. In a lot of small things I made myself as agreeable and thoughtful as possible. I consciously put Norman's needs ahead of my own. Finally this paid off, because six months later, out of the blue, Norman suddenly said to me, 'Ruth, I know how much you love that old farm house in Pawling. I've been thinking. Maybe we could get a mortgage and somehow borrow the rest of the money. . . . "

They purchased the property and named it "Sugar Tree Farm" in honor of the small town in Ohio where Dr. Peale's parents lived. When their children were younger, the family spent all summer at the farm; during the school year, however, the only time they could get to Pawling was from after school on Friday to Saturday evening.

Dr. and Mrs. Peale no longer own "Sugar Hill Farm," for in recent years they have moved to a neighboring place called "Hill Farm." Here, with no barn to obstruct the view, they can watch the shadows gather across the Catskill Mountains and the valleys, at least on the rare occasions their busy schedule allows. "Hill Farm" is described by Mrs. Peale as "one of those old Pawling houses you buy to fix up." And with her usual flair, Mrs. Peale "fixed up" the home, giving it warmth and charm. It is tastefully decorated with Scandinavian antiques and beautiful Oriental rugs.

The farm in Pawling has been a place of inspiration for Peale. He says, "Whenever I am depressed or discouraged, something in me instinctively turns to the land. Even if the troubles do not go away, something in my soul almost always finds the strength and serenity to endure this period."

Today leisure time in their Pawling home is more of a dream for the Peales than a reality. They are just too busy to spend much time there. They regularly schedule time for Pawling but usually something comes up to prevent them from going. And when they do get to Pawling? Peale explains how it is. "When people hear that we've gone to Pawling they think we go there to luxuriate in our country home. Now here are the plain facts. We go to Pawling and we go to the Foundation for Christian Living office and work there all day long! Then we go home and have an early dinner and are in bed by 9 or 9:30 P.M. Next morning we're down at the office again at 9 A.M., or we go to Carmel which is eighteen miles away, and work all day at *Guideposts*. Or we go down to radio station WPUT where we use a recording studio and spend two or three hours recording. So when people say, 'Oh, you're going to Pawling,' it's not what they think!

"We bought that place originally for the purpose which people think we did, to have a country home, a place to escape to. But immediately we established these organizations contingent to it. So it became just like our residence in the city and associated with our work. Our apartment in the city is for my office there and the church. Our house in Pawling is for the 'FCL' office and the *Guideposts* office at Carmel. That's what it is. It happens to be in the country whereas the apartment residence is in the city, but we don't get time to enjoy the country that much.

"The only way we could have a country place would be to go fifty miles further north where we have no occupation. Then what we would do is establish another organization there! That's the way we are!"

The account Mrs. Peale gives of a day at Pawling is hardly any different. Mrs. Peale claims she is an early riser and a "fast starter" whereas her husband is a late riser and a "slow starter"—in this case a late riser being defined as one who gets up at 7 A.M.

A typical day at Pawling for Ruth Peale is to get up an hour before her husband wakes up and begin the day by editing for print the sermons which Peale has previously preached at Marble Collegiate Church. Ruth's challenge is to turn the spoken word into a smooth reading manuscript for publication.

At 7:30 A.M. or so Ruth sticks the wash in and begins getting breakfast. There is no hired help in the house. Work begins in earnest over breakfast, discussing what speaking engagements to accept and preparing the Peales' newspaper column "There's an Answer!" By 9 A.M. or so the dishes have been washed, the beds made, the wash in the dryer put away, lunches made, and the Peales, briefcases in hand, set off for their offices at the Foundation for Christian Living. There, they head to their adjoining offices where throughout the day they will consult each other frequently on different matters. Peale starts writing, dictating letters, and returning phone calls while his wife plunges into a two hour policy meeting with executives and supervisors of 'FCL.' After lunch she drives over to Sugar Hill Farm for a babysitting stint with her grandchildren, and then it's back to the office and business as usual. The Peales work independently, occasionally conferring with each other by phone or in person, until the office closes at 4 P.M. But they continue to work, feeling they can get more done in the quiet of the deserted offices. So goes a typical day with the Peales, "relaxing" at Pawling!

Elizabeth Peale Allen says, "Mother and Daddy are working as hard as ever—that will never change —but with us kids out of the way they are able to travel everywhere together, and they do a great deal of that.

"When they're at home, I notice that they like to putter around the house more than they used to. There are no servants; they don't want anybody serving them. Mother cooks. Simple things: hamburgers, chicken on the spit, leg of lamb. They like gadgets; they get them, but don't use them. And they like good cars and hotels. But their tastes are midwestern and plain, and although they have known splendor and elegance—staying overnight at the White House, say, or visiting the Chiang Kai-sheks in Taiwan—they've never been changed by it."

Elizabeth continues, "There are times when I feel a touch of sadness for them. They both like people so much, yet they don't have many close friends. They have old friends that they have kept in touch with, but they don't have what you might call 'buddies.' I've said that to Mother, and she has said that as a minister and wife in a large church they couldn't, they shouldn't be selective with their friends. Anyway, with their schedule, there wasn't time for purely social contact. But people are their lives. And people fill their lives."

No one can question that Peale is successful, and that with his successes have come the material things he needs for his busy life. With this has come criticism from those who think, by some strange reasoning, that all ministers should be poor as church mice.

The Peales drive a maroon and gold Cadillac Seville. If they can afford it, which they certainly can, they deserve it. It is really nobody's business but their own, yet this is the type of thing that reporters seize and hold up apparently for criticism. How Peale came to buy his first Cadillac tells a lot about him and his attitudes toward his success and the resultant wealth.

Rev. Ralph Lankler was pastor of Christ Church, the little church the Peales support and and attend while in Pawling. Peale has sometimes called Lankler his pastor. Both clergymen were at the meeting of the Pawling Rotary Club. Lankler left early. Before leaving he told Peale he was driving to Poughkeepsie, a good drive from Pawling, to see a man in the hospital who was one of the poorest and also least-respected people in Pawling. Peale tells what happened.

"As Ralph drove away a visiting Rotarian, who knew Lankler was a minister because Ralph had given the invocation, said, 'Look at that minister driving a Cadillac!' Well that really reeked me! I said to the man, 'Now let me tell you something, my friend. That man you just saw driving away in that Cadillac spends his entire life helping the poor and needy. He is on his way now to the hospital in Poughkeepsie to see a man who isn't even a member of his church.' Well, I gave him a long speech about Ralph Lankler, his goodness, his self-sacrificing spirit, and everything. I didn't lose my temper, but I was very firm and everybody in the Rotary Club heard my lecture. Then I said, 'It's nobody's business but his if he drives a Cadillac.' I was really fired up! So I added, 'Now, I'm going to tell you something, I'm going right out now and get a Cadillac for myself. I don't care what you think about it! Why do you criticize a minister? What do you drive?' Well, it wasn't much of a conversation, but at the same time, it made the point. And I got a Cadillac. It's so silly! Who cares? It's all right to drive one if you can afford it."

The Peales candidly attribute their success in life and the financial success that they have received to the goodness and provision of the Lord. Since Peale got through seminary by working and borrowing money, by the time he became pastor in Syracuse he was paying off his own educational debts and at the same time putting his younger brother through school.

Peale doesn't see anything wrong with success or having the money to provide all the offices and help he needs to do his job well. But he doesn't equate success with money. He says, "Some of the greatest failures I've known in my life have been wealthy people. Some have been terrible failures in their personality, the way they handled life, or how they dealt with their families. Others have been successes. I knew one man who told me, 'I've only got one gift and that is that I can make money. I don't know why I can make money, but I can. Outside of that I'm nobody.' So he said, 'The only way I can square it with God is to give away as much as I can. Because if God gave me the gift to make money, He must want me to make it for some good purpose.' So the money passed through this man and on to someone else. He lived very simply. I would call him a success! He was a success because he handled money, the money didn't handle him. But I've known some other people who let the money handle them and I regard these people as failures."

For Peale, success is part of the American way in that it creates prosperity. He says, "What's wrong with a man going into business, becoming successful in business and a leader in the community and in the church? I see nothing wrong with that! Wherever you've got a man who is successful financially and interested in his community, when he builds a business that business puts wealth into the community, it helps thousands of people. If he wasn't there to build the factory there would be no jobs for people. He's part of an economy that flows.

"There are some people who've made lots of money but who in my opinion certainly aren't successful; but there are others who have been very great successes. I've known poor people who are more successful than people who have money because they know how to manage their own personal lives."

Success for Norman Vincent Peale might be described as a mutual love affair with life, people, and God.

The Making of a Positive Thinker

It was a strain for Charles and Anna Peale to send their son to Ohio Wesleyan University; but Charles had always wished that he had gone to Ohio Wesleyan and he wanted that opportunity for his son. As he left his son at the University, Charles Peale took him aside and delivered some man-to-man advice: "Study hard, stay away from liquor, don't smoke, and don't run around with women." Just the kind of advice you'd expect from a Methodist minister. Then he added, a bit more gently, "But if you do get into trouble, don't lie about it or try to hide it. Just come and tell me and I'll see what I can do to help you get through."

Peale, like most freshmen, found that kind of parental advice hard to live up to. He recalls, "It was not just 'Don't drink' or 'Don't smoke,' prohibitions that were and are valid for many good reasons. It was also 'Don't play cards' and 'Don't dance' and 'Don't go to the theater' and 'Don't do anything enjoyable on Sunday.' We lived under a form of Puritanism, really, stern and well-intentioned, but also naive. Cards were equated with gambling, and dancing with orgies, and the theater meant vice and fallen women. As late as the turn of the century, it is said a student was actually expelled from my college, Ohio Wesleyan, for going to see a Shakespearean play. Anything as repressive and narrow-minded as this was bound to bring about a rebellion against purely negative rules. And it did."

Peale smoked in college for a while before deciding that he was not going to let the craving for nicotine control him. So he quit and has remained a non-smoker. He was also known to occasionally indulge in a little elderberry wine. But that form of rebellion didn't last long and since then Peale has been a lifelong temperance advocate.

Like most freshmen, the most important things Peale was learning that first year were not to be found in textbooks. The course at Ohio Wesleyan required little science or math and stressed English, history, religion, and economics. Two languages were required, one modern and one ancient. That first year Norman Vincent Peale earned one A in speech; and in Greek and gym he got straight F's. But the main things that Norman learned that year had to do with his own independence, who he was, what he was about, and what he wanted to become.

When he entered college, Peale was plagued by self-consciousness. In spite of the A he received for extemporaneous speaking, whenever he was called on to speak he felt self-conscious and inadequate. His speech teacher finally confronted Peale with the real cause of the problem—Peale's self-centeredness. Only then was Peale able to adequately analyze the situation. Sitting on the steps of the college chapel, he asked the Lord to help him to get his life together and not to be so wrapped up in his own self and inadequacies. This was a turning point in his life.

His friend from college, Raymond Thornberg, recalls, "He was a very forceful figure, even as an undergraduate; not a 'wheel' in the sense of being president of the student body, though he seemed to be involved in everything. I can see him now, standing on the chapel steps, a group around him as usual; he talking, they listening. Sometimes I'd stand at a distance and watch the way his college friends would pay attention to him. And yet, Norman himself has told me that he had an inferiority complex. Strange. There must be a very dim and confusing line between inferiority feelings and humility."

Peale recalls one day when he went as a delegate to a youth organization called the Student Volunteers. "It was a spiritually oriented movement and was composed of some pretty dedicated and enthusiastic college young people. Indeed, this movement had swept the college campuses of America with a strong religious impulse.

On the occasion of Norman Peale's 40th anniversary as the pastor of Marble Collegiate Church, he is joined by his son-in-law Rev. Hall Everitt (far left), his son, Rev. John Peale (on Peale's right), and his brother, Rev. Leonard Peale (on Peale's left).

"The great hall was packed to capacity. The atmosphere was charged with powerful emotional feelings. As I entered the hall I stopped short in my tracks, for stretched across the stage high enough for the enormous audience to see was a huge sign which read, 'The Evangelization of the World in This Generation.'

"Something about the audacity, the consummate nerve of that slogan, hit my mind with a powerful impulse. At that moment I experienced an inner response so deep in content that I knew what I had to do in life, what down deep I wanted to do. I had my goal instantly formed, which was to do all that I could by whatever means to persuade and persuade and persuade people that they have built within them God-given and fantastic powers that, when released, can and will revamp them into significant personalities."

Peale enjoyed his involvement on the college newspaper, *The Ohio Wesleyan Transcript,* and even more on the *Findlay* (Ohio) *Morning Republican.* He decided that this would be the vehicle through which he would fulfill his newfound goal in life. He began to become more and more enthused about the newspaper business, even at one time dreaming dreams of building a Peale newspaper empire. The newspaper was a way to influence and mold thought, and perhaps even a stepping-stone to a political career. And yet there was something in Peale, something deeply ingrained in his background which never enabled him to completely rule out the ministry.

Growing up in the home of a minister, Peale knew all the disadvantages of the profession. Peale recalls one of the most embarrassing moments of his life which for many years contributed to his feelings of inferiority. He shares the feeling of many preachers as well. "In my boyhood days in small Ohio towns, the local banker was always the leading citizen, the authentic 'big shot' so to say. I remember he lived in the biggest house on the main street. His residence sat back among the wide lawns and venerable trees. His driveway swept through the big impressive gates up to a stately portico. In my early boyhood, the pompous banker rode regally behind a spanking pair of matched horses downtown each morning, home to lunch, to town again, and back for supper. And of course he was the first in town to chug down Main Street in an automobile. It was all

very impressive, right down to his big desk which could be seen through the bank window before which there was much bowing and scraping of all and sundry in whom he literally owned shares. This included just about everyone in town.

"On Monday mornings I would often accompany my preacher father to the bank where the banker, as treasurer of our church, would pay him his weekly salary. Awestruck, I would follow Dad into the great man's office, my heart thumping, hands sweating. It cut deeply into my supersensitive young nature to hear the banker get off his threadbare witticism: 'Well, brother Peale, do you think your sermon of yesterday justifies your pay?' This always riled me. But my father, mature and urbane, gracefully carried off the weekly joviality. He knew it wasn't ill-meant. But as for me I was afraid of bankers for years."

Peale resented the subtle and not-so-subtle pressure from the "big wigs" of the congregation who lived by a double standard: a grand lifestyle for them and the lifestyle of a pauper for the preacher. Like most pastors' families, the Peales seldom ate out and when they did the most important item on the menu was the price. Things that other young people received as a matter of course, sports equipment and the like, could not be afforded in the Peale household. Peale determined that when he grew up he would not be poor. If this meant that he could not be a minister, then so be it. Certainly Peale was not the first, nor the last, to feel that sentiment.

It did not have to be this way. Norman's father, Charles Peale, had been trained as a medical doctor and had built up a good reputation in medicine, serving at one time as the chief public health officer for the city of Milwaukee. Before he had met and married Anna Peale, the elder Peale suffered a serious illness. It was touch and go for a while and he barely survived. When it became apparent that he would recover, his mother said to him, "The Lord has spared your life. I think he has his reasons. What do you think?" In that emotional moment Charles Peale had a tremendous spiritual experience. He concluded that, "I owe my life to the Lord. I'll give it to him. I'll stop being a doctor. I'll be a minister." And so he gave up the lucrative profession of being a doctor for the meager income of a country parson.

Like most children, Peale wanted to be all sorts of things. First he wanted to be a shortstop for the

*Peale preaches an enthusiastic sermon on Easter Sunday
at Marble.*

Cincinnati Reds. About the same time he was taking piano lessons from his aunt who had visions of him playing at Carnegie Hall. Then, listening to trains whistling through the Ohio night, he wanted to be a railroad engineer. He also thought about following in his father's footsteps. One rainy afternoon his mother found young Norman standing in the pulpit of the empty church preaching to the pews, imitating his father's gestures and pulpit style.

Like most children he hated spinach and algebra but loved the circus. Unlike most children he was a preacher's child. Whether he liked it or not this meant that he was different and that frequently there was a double standard of behavior. One standard for ordinary kids—the "OK's"—and another standard for preacher's kids—the "PK's." Like most preacher's kids the Peale brothers were sometimes infuriated by such a double standard and felt obliged to go to lengths to prove how normal they really were. All children must go through a stage of rebellion but for preacher's children it is *de rigueur*. It's just that more is expected of preacher's kids; so Norman went to a store, bought a nickel cigar, and sauntered down the street smoking it—only to walk smack into his father.

Peale developed a self-consciousness and sense of inferiority and inadequacy which haunted him for many years. Part of his insecurity was related to being a preacher's kid and the demands which that placed upon him. He recalls, "My two younger brothers and I refused to be sissies. In order to camouflage our sensitiveness about being preacher's sons, we would sometimes do stunts like smoking cigarettes behind the barn or racing down Main Street in our father's Reo. It was even rumored in the town that we would come to no good end.

"In school, also, I was awed by overbright, cocky, loudmouthed students who seemingly could talk glibly on any subject. As for myself, I was shy and reticent and rather inarticulate for the most part. I knew the subject matter but expressed it poorly. If any other student laughed or smiled as I spoke, I froze immediately. So I gave way in my own thoughts before these smug fellow students who cockily acted as if they had all the answers. I believed that they were all far ahead of me in ability, and so I was afraid of them.

"But this fear was indeed difficult for me to overcome; that awestruck fear of the prominent or well-known or those with money or position. I felt inferior and inadequate in the presence of anyone who threw his weight around."

A lot of Peale's inferiority complex can be traced back to the fact that he didn't have a lot of weight to throw around. "As a small boy I was painfully thin. I had lots of energy, was on the track team, was healthy and hard as nails, but thin. And that bothered me because I didn't want to be thin. I wanted to be fat. I was called 'skinny' but I didn't want to be called 'skinny.' I wanted to be called 'fat.' I longed to be hard-boiled and tough and fat. I did everything to get fat. I drank cod liver oil, consumed vast numbers of milk shakes, ate thousands of chocolate sundaes with whipped cream and nuts, cakes and pies innumerable, but they did not affect me in the slightest. I stayed thin and lay awake nights thinking and agonizing about it. I kept on trying to get heavy until I was about thirty, when all of a sudden I did get heavy! I bulged at the seams. Then I became self-conscious because I was so fat, and finally had to take off forty pounds with equal agony to get myself down to respectable size."

In spite of his adolescent rebellion, Peale loved and respected his father. He recalls as a child riding to church in a horse and buggy dashing through snowdrifts as the cold whipped across the barren Ohio farmland. When he observed what a miserable night it was, young Norman received a sermon from his dad on "The Glory and Might of the Storm." Norman remembers, "He dwelt upon the power of the elements, the lonely loveliness of the landscape. He pictured the snug warmth inside the little farmhouses along the way with blue smoke rising from the kitchen fires. He was a great preacher and I loved to hear him talk to a congregation. He was thrilling because he was himself always thrilled. But never did I hear him in better form than that winter twilight as he delivered a sermon on the majesty of nature in a snowstorm to one little boy in a buggy on a country road.

"When later after the service, Duck, our horse floundered us home, the storm had ceased and a full moon lighted up the whole countryside in silvery radiance. Dad gave me another talk on how storms always pass and 'the glory of God shines through.' Dad saw God in everything. Maybe that was the source of his amazing enthusiasm. As we drove up the lane to put Duck in the barn he said something I've never forgotten: 'Always make yourself enthusiastic, Norman, and your whole life will be wonderful.' "

Although impressed by his father's powerful preaching and influence on people's lives, including the changed lives that he saw in the community as a result of his father's preaching, Peale was nonetheless turned off to the ministry as a possible vocation. He resented the tendency of people to set his father apart from other men because he was a minister, and even more resented the demands that his father's profession had placed on him. He vowed that the one thing he would never do was to become a preacher.

For a while he became a young salesman of newly invented aluminum pots and pans. He memorized his sales pitch and took the interurban train to Union City, Indiana, where he began his career as a salesman. With great enthusiasm, aluminum pots in hand, and memorized sales pitch, he approached the first house and knocked on the door. When the lady of the house answered, her hair up in curlers, a broom in one hand and a dustpan in the other, Norman's confidence evaporated. He backed off asking, "You didn't want to buy any pots and pans did you?" Naturally, the lady agreed and slammed the door.

The next day, Peale teamed up with a friend who supported him in his selling, a lesson which has paid off handsomely for Peale, if not in commissions from the sale of pots and pans, then in honorariums from the thousands of speaking engagements Peale has had at sales conventions. The magic formula was simple: believe in yourself, believe in your product, find the need of your customer and fill it.

Although disappointed that their son was not going to follow in his father's footsteps, the Peales were determined to let Norman make his own decisions. Following college he went to work as a string reporter for the *Findlay Morning Republican* where he was given the lowliest beat on the paper—the obituaries. It was not the most exciting introduction to the world of journalism; but Peale persisted and after a few months on the *Republican* he landed a job with the *Detroit Journal*. Peale moved to Detroit and lived at the local Y.M.C.A. while serving as a cub reporter. He covered such things as conferences, conventions, trials, and service club luncheons, preferably something where a free meal went with the assignment.

From the managing editor, Grove Patterson, Norman learned a number of lessons which profoundly changed his life and influenced his later career. At one time the editor asked Peale that if he were covering a political convention, how would he slant his copy—for a college professor or a ditch digger? Peale learned. Much of the success of his ministry is due to the basic lesson that he learned from Grove Patterson. Peale's messages and writings have always been slanted to the average man.

From Grove Patterson, young Norman Vincent Peale learned perhaps the greatest lesson in his life: the secret of overcoming his feelings of inadequacy and inferiority. Peale recalls, "When I was a young reporter on the old *Detroit Journal*, my editor, Grove Patterson, took a kindly interest in me, a young man fresh out of college and working on a

metropolitan newspaper. He was a man of keen, perceptive insights. One day he called me to his office. He could always make one feel at ease even though he was top man on the paper and his visitor in this case was the lowliest."

Peale wasn't exactly a great success in the newspaper business. Perhaps he would have been, but he certainly didn't set the journalistic world on fire. Actually, he was young and did not stay with it long enough to determine what he might have been in this field.

The decision to leave the newspaper business did not come easily or quickly. Lurking within Peale's inner being, underneath any resentment he felt toward being a preacher's kid and toward some of the ways in which ministers were treated, there was still the desire to communicate Christ's gospel and love. And there was the deep impression that had been made on him by his father and his upbringing in the Methodist church. The matter was brought to a head when Peale heard of another newspaper job in Troy, Ohio, which could have provided a major stepping stone for him. On the way to check it out, he stopped at his hometown to visit his parents. While attending church, his suppressed urge to become a minister welled up within him. After the evening service he took a long walk, wrestling with his future. He asked the Lord to show him what He wanted him to do. Peale prayed, "I'm willing to do whatever You want me to do. Help me to make the right decision. Send me a sign." But there were no flashes of lightning streaking across the sky and no booming voice from heaven. So Peale began weighing the situation in his mind, evaluating all the problems involved, all of the uncertainties, all of the questions. Unable to resolve the dilemma, he decided to proceed with caution, not irrevocably committing himself to the ministry, but at least sticking his toe in the water. He decided to apply for admission to Boston University and work toward a Master of Arts degree in the graduate school while, at the same time, taking some courses at the divinity school. That would give him a sampling without making the total commitment. And it would give the Lord the opportunity to lead him in whatever direction he was to go. On the way home that night Peale again prayed, "All right, Lord, I've put one toe in. I'm sorry, but it's the best I can do. The rest is up to You."

Reverend Mister Peale

Peale's choice of Boston University was logical for a graduate of Ohio Wesleyan University. He moved to Boston living and working at the Y.M.C.A. Earning his way through Boston University by working in the kitchen at the "Y", he earned the grand sum of $2 a day plus board.

In addition to his regular studies at the University, Peale became a prolific reader, a practice which he has maintained to this day. It was during this period that Peale discovered psychologist William James who has influenced Peale's thinking perhaps more than anyone else except Jesus Christ. James is quoted more often by Peale in his writing than anyone else except maybe Emerson. Peale worked concurrently on two degrees, a Master of Arts with a major in ethics at Boston University Graduate School and a Bachelor of Sacred Theology in the University's Divinity School. The resistance to the ministry was steadily eroding.

In the second semester of his first year at the University came the opportunity to put his calling to the test: Peale was invited to preach in the Methodist church in Walpole, Massachusetts.

He began two weeks of feverish preparation. He chose as his text his father's favorite verse and a text which has become his own favorite, "I am come that they might have life, and that they might have it more abundantly." Peale wrote and rewrote, and rewrote again, preparing at least seven versions of the sermon. Each one seemed to be lacking and ended up in the trash can. He couldn't seem to find just the right words, phrases, and illustrations to communicate the point he wanted to make. Worse yet, he wasn't at all sure he even knew what the point was that he wanted to make; and perhaps that was part of the problem.

Finally, in desperation, he telegraphed his father asking for notes on one of his dad's old sermons. His father wired back, "Prepare your own sermon! Just tell people that Jesus Christ can change their lives!"

He remembered the advice of his professor, George S. Butters, who had told his students, "Just keep it simple. In order to preach effectively you have to get in there and love the congregation." So he started all over again preparing the sermon one more time.

He reached the tiny church determined to do his best and give a profound and inspiring sermon. He went into a little room behind the pulpit to wait and take a last minute look at his sermon notes when he happened to look out the window. Lo and behold there were people coming into the church! People! Somehow it had all seemed easier when he was rehearsing his sermon in the privacy of his room looking in the mirror. But actually standing up in front of people and delivering it was something totally different! The old inadequacies of his youth began to sweep over him and his knees began to shake, his confidence gone.

In his panic, he did the only thing that he could do under the circumstances; he fell to his knees beside an old red couch in the room and unburdened himself to the Lord. In desperation he asked the Lord to help him say something that would help those people. Peale says, "Suddenly, I had a great sense of peace in my mind and heart and then a very moving impression of the presence of Jesus. It was as if He said to me, 'Do not be anxious. Simply tell the people what you know about me and remind them that I will help them if they will give their lives to me.' This experience was so overpowering that I feel its reality to this very day. It was followed by a great sense of exultation, and then there dawned in my mind a great longing that still surges through my soul. It was this: I wanted with all my heart to do everything I possibly could to get everybody, everywhere, to realize how much they needed Jesus, and to know by personal experience what he could mean in their lives."

This was the turning point in Peale's life, the moment that he made up his mind to become a preacher. "At that moment I embarked on a crusade. In fact, I remember saying out loud that I would consecrate my humble talents and abilities in my lifetime to doing everything possible to get all the people in the United States to accept Jesus Christ and to live the life which he came to teach about."

The crisis was over. Peale forgot all about his carefully prepared notes and just stood there sharing with the congregation what Christ meant to him, and how Christ's power could flood their lives if they let him. He pointed out that they were meant for God, and that only God could fulfill the deepest longings of their lives. The sermon lasted only twelve minutes but it made its point. He knew it. It was something he could feel standing in the pulpit looking out at the audience talking to them. He was not just talking to them, he was communicating with them, touching them where they were at. He felt warm, fulfilled, and elated.

But on the train back to Boston the old doubts set in. Critically he evaluated his performance. Twelve minutes! How on earth was he going to preach fifty-two sermons a year for the rest of his life if he couldn't come up with enough material to last more than twelve minutes? He had other questions. He explains, "You see, I had studied in Boston University School of Theology where they didn't go in for any such simple kind of faith. They pooh-poohed stories of naive souls who put a trusting faith in the Lord to help them in practical affairs and were sustained thereby. The so-called faith element in religion they just couldn't see at all; the main thing was an ethically patterned Christianity designed to facilitate the rise of the left-wing panaceas which they smugly called 'intellectually respectable' religion.

"They were good men who taught and studied there, and many of them had come out of the homes of old-fashioned plain people; and while they had a tender nostalgia for the uncomplicated faith of their fathers, they had proceeded so far into religious and sociological sophistication that the idea of God helping anybody in a way that smacked of the supernatural to any extent was considered reactionary. And, of course, I went for this assuredly 'intellectual' point of view, hook, line and sinker."

Peale thought about these things staring out the window as the train raced back to Boston. But the Lord had gotten him through that first sermon, so who was he to doubt that the Lord would be able to get him through all the others to come.

Peale had other opportunities that year to go out and preach on what seminary students call the "circuit"—usually churches too small to afford their own ministers, or churches temporarily without a pastor. The only way to learn to preach is to preach; and with each sermon, Norman's confidence and skill improved. In some of these little churches Peale would stay with members of the congregation and usually the woman of the house would try to fatten him up with a big Sunday dinner. Other times he stayed in little small town hotels like the one in Hancock, New Hampshire, where in winter it was so cold that the water in the wash basin would freeze solid during the night. That summer Norman went back to Ohio and had the opportunity to preach in one of the local Methodist churches. He was determined to make good use of his education and so worked at great length producing a sermon which gave ample evidence of all the theology he had learned. He recalls the title was "The Kinetic Theory of the Atonement"—"or something like that, something I thought I knew then, but I don't know now.

"I've always had a photographic memory of things. Instances that happened years ago are as real to me today as the day they happened. I can see my father sitting on the front porch of our house in Findlay scrutinizing that sermon and then propping his feet up on the porch rail, leaning back, popping peanuts into his mouth, and telling me what a lousy sermon it was, then giving me some good solid advice on preaching."

Peale's father gave him basic lessons in homiletics. From his dad Peale learned not to take a manuscript into the pulpit but to deliver his sermon extemporaneously. His dad concluded, "In your desire to impress people with your own profundity, you seem to have forgotten that the way to the human heart is through simplicity."

Peale was crestfallen. Charles Peale went on to give his son the same advice which John Wesley had offered centuries earlier, and the same advice which Peale later gave to me. His dad said, "Simply tell them—*simply* tell them—how Christ has helped you, and how he will help them if they will just give him a chance. That's the greatest message in the world, that's the only message you'll ever need. Just tell the people that, keep telling them that, and they'll break down the doors to get into your church to hear the message."

While still in the seminary Peale was assigned to his first church in Berkeley, Rhode Island, as a student pastor. It was a long way from Fifth Avenue; Peale had to do most of the janitor's duties himself. But his duties didn't include cleaning the restrooms because there were none. This serious deficiency in the church was remedied when the young Reverend Peale found an abandoned outhouse. The owner willingly gave it to the church. Peale organized the men of the church and the outhouse was lifted onto a borrowed truck and driven to the church with the Reverend Mister Peale perched triumphantly on top! What they didn't teach you in seminary! But the church had more serious problems than its lack of a privy. Half of the church was set against the other half, the result of a bitter strike in the textile town. The mill owners were on one side of the dispute and the workers on the other. Peale recalls that half of the people sat on one side of the main aisle and glared at the other half across the aisle. Although his sympathies were with the workers, Peale sought to mediate between the two sides and bring the power of Christian love to bear on the situation. Frequently he visited the factory owners on behalf of the workers presenting their grievances.

It was here that Peale determined to preach what he calls "evangelistic" sermons. Not everyone has recognized his sermons as evangelistic because he doesn't use the traditional language but nevertheless this is what they are. "It was the custom in those days to invite people to come to the altar to accept Christ and confess him publicly. And it is still good to get people to the point of making an actual decision, to break with the past, and to look toward Christ and accept him as a powerful influence in changing their thought pattern and thus changing their life. It was and is also beneficial to step out courageously before one's fellows, confess one's new faith and say publicly, 'This is the way I'm going to live!' I still have a great faith in the healing power of the altar where one kneels to pray and to surrender oneself to the Lord . . . " The first night that Peale gave an altar call, five people came forward and knelt at the altar. He vividly remembers that night and walking home impressed by the power of God. He says, "I began to work in this field both in preaching and in private interview. I became amazed by the wonderful truth that if a man began to think differently and wanted to be different and would have faith and would surrender, his life could be changed. I saw people whose lives were very bad become very good people. I saw those who were haunted by fear and inferiority and all kinds of defeat turn to Christ and begin to live His way and become changed. I developed an unbounded conviction that continues to this moment: there is

nobody whose life cannot be changed who will let Christ change it. Anybody can live a better life if he really wants to and will pay the price of separating himself in his mind, by desire and by faith, from that which formerly defeated him. The man himself doesn't do it. Christ does it. But when one surrenders, then Christ will do it."

After graduating from Boston University, Peale's first church was in Brooklyn, in a newly developing area on the corner of East 37th Street and Kings Highway. The Flatlands Methodist Church was a tiny building with virtually no congregation. It was run down, surrounded by overgrown lots filled with rubbish and broken bottles. Peale says, "There was no way to go but up!" Attendance had dwindled to forty people per week and the sexton was actually chopping up unused pews for use as firewood!

Peale began going door to door inviting new families in the area and those without any church affiliation to attend his church. He built up a mailing list and worked it weekly. Combining folksiness, friendliness, sentimentalism, patriotism, and old-fashioned revivalism, Peale advertised to build up the church in membership and attendance. In six months, the tiny church was packed and Peale was forced to move his congregation to a revival-time canvas tent while they raised money to build a new church.

The message wasn't new—it was the same old gospel his dad had preached back in Ohio, but the old vocabulary was gone. Peale was communicating the ageless gospel in a contemporary and fresh way. The packaging was different, the message was the same. Peale stood out from the pulpiteers of his day. According to a fortieth anniversary booklet issued by Marble Collegiate Church many years later, "He was self-deprecating, humorous. His sermons were filled with wonderful stories that were like carrots dangling in a rabbit trap; his audience nibbled away unsuspectingly until wham! The gates slid down and suddenly they found themselves trapped in the spiritual point Norman had intended for them all along." Today, basically nothing has changed! That's still the way Peale preaches.

When he left the Flatlands Church only three years later, a new building had been erected and the membership of the church had swelled to over nine hundred people. Peale was the right man, in the right place, at the right time, communicating a message that people were anxious to hear. Not surprisingly, this put him at a premium and he was called to the University Church of Syracuse, New York.

The Syracuse church was a prestigious congregation attended by many of the students and faculty of Syracuse University. It was a stately old building, and even though mostly empty, it represented a great challenge and opportunity for the twenty-eight year old Reverend Peale, as well as a small increase in salary.

It took Peale a while to adjust to the congregation. He was impressed and somewhat intimidated by all the Ph.D.'s from the University who sat in the pews each Sunday. He felt compelled to upgrade the intellectual content of his own preaching.

"I knew I was in a university pulpit and therefore I thought I had to preach very scholarly sermons," says Peale. "I attempted to do that. I read heavy books and quoted learned authority. In fact I tried to preach a baccalaureate sermon every Sunday morning. One day, one of the most outstanding intellectual members of the faculty took me out to lunch. He was gracious and kind, and told me that he wanted to help in every way he could. Then he said, 'I would like to make a little suggestion. You think that we being college professors, want an intellectualized sermon. Now,' he said, 'you must remember something about us. We may be experts in our fields; one man in biology, another in geology, another in history. You must be an expert in the field of the Spirit. You must realize, when we come down to listen to you on Sunday, that we look up to you as the teacher, and you must tell us what you,

personally, know about this, not what somebody said about it in a book that you are going to quote.

" 'And remember this,' he said, 'We are all men and women who need God. We're just poor sinful people and you mustn't be so awed by us that you cannot tell us directly wherein we are wrong and need repentance. Preach to us the same as you would anybody else.' "

Like most ministers, Peale didn't enjoy preaching to empty pews! He was particularly irked by all the empty pews in Syracuse. And it seemed as if no one ever expected them to be filled. Each Sunday from the pulpit he would look up into the balcony and see a huge ladder lying across the balcony pews. He asked the sexton why the ladder was there and the man replied, "It's the best place to keep it because nobody ever sits there."

Peale recalls, "Every Sunday, that ladder annoyed me. I didn't want to preach to a ladder. I wanted to preach to human beings. We couldn't save the world with a ladder!" So Peale embarked on a campaign to fill the church. He worked almost nonstop. He put to work some of the advertising and promotional techniques he had used back in Brooklyn. He built his mailing list and began working it each week sending out cards, tantalizing people with cleverly-worded invitations to church. The cards asked questions like, "Why is it suddenly hard to get a seat at the University Church?" It wasn't exactly true, because there were lots of seats up in the balcony with the ladder. But it wasn't really false either. In Peale's mind he could already see the church filled so he was only telling the truth in advance. The tactic worked and before long Peale was packing the church.

This was back in the days when commercial radio had just come into being and Peale began a weekly radio program called, "The Angelus Hour." He began giving lectures wherever anyone would listen, working with a lecture bureau who, under the heading "Peale's Appeal", promised, "Poetry, philosophy, literature and all the sciences in an amazing roll call, are called upon to testify to the worth of personality." Peale was on his way!

People flocked to Peale's church including a good number of coeds from Syracuse University. At twenty-eight, wearing a swallow-tailed morning coat, speaking authoritatively, waving his arms, and holding the audience in the palm of his hand, Peale had to have been an attraction for the ladies of the

The University United Methodist Church in Syracuse, New York, (Peale's second church after graduation).

town! He was the well-known pastor of the largest church in town, living well in bachelor's quarters at the Syracuse Hotel, and even at one point referred to by the *Syracuse Post-Standard* as "Syracuse's most eligible bachelor."

The story of Peale's eligibility, his romance, and subsequent marriage to Ruth Stafford has been told in Peale's authorized biography, *Minister to Millions* by Arthur Gordon. This book became the basis for a Hollywood movie about the life of Peale called *One Man's Way*, released by United Artists and starring Don Murray. Peale laughs off the romanticism of his courtship with Ruth Stafford and the movie's portrayal as a bit extravagant. I replied, "You weren't quite a catch?"

"I wouldn't say so. No, I don't see why."

So I asked, "Was Ruth quite a catch for you?"

With positive enthusiasm he replied, "Oh yes! She was for me. I thought so! She was quite a popular girl then."

Ruth and Norman met one night at a party given by the church's young people's group. Her roommate introduced them and Ruth remembers that Norman held her hand what seemed to be just a little longer than necessary. Peale had to pursue this young coed with care, because, obviously, there were lots of other girls in the congregation vying for his attention and he had his reputation as a minister to protect. He began very indirectly, telephoning her to invite her back to church, getting her involved on various youth committees within the church, and inventing occasions to see her on "official church business." After working on a dinner together, Peale engineered the head table so that he and Ruth Stafford would sit together.

Dinner alone followed. The two began doing many things together, working together, sharing ideas and friendship. He even asked Ruth to start critiquing his sermons, asking her to be very frank and honest. But when she was, Peale wasn't always prepared for her honesty.

They tried to be discreet, but eventually word of their deepening relationship spread around. Some of the members of the congregation were delighted! After all every good minister should also have a good minister's wife! There were others who were not so enthusiastic. Perhaps they thought they were more suited for the position of Mrs. Norman Vincent Peale than Ruth Stafford.

The relationship continued and deepened until

The interior of the University United Methodist Church

one evening Norman went over to the sorority house where Ruth served as manager and handed her a ring box saying, "It didn't cost much, but it says, 'I love you!' " Their engagement lasted for two years. Neither was financially able to consider marriage immediately after Ruth's graduation from college. Peale was still paying off the debts for his own education and helping his brother through school. And Norman's family was not at all sure that Ruth Stafford was the right girl for their son. But love won out and two years after her graduation Ruth Stafford and Norman Peale were joined in marriage at University Church. It was a warm, June day with the ceremony conducted by Norman's father, Bishop Adna W. Leonard, and Chancellor Charles W. Flint of Syracuse University. It was one of the biggest social events of the year, and as the newlywed couple drove away from the church, Peale leaned over to his new bride and whispered, "What a crowd! If we could only have taken up an offering!" After a group honeymoon, an unusual arrangement in which Peale's parents accompanied the newlyweds, the young Reverend Peale and his bride returned to take up their duties in Syracuse.

The church flourished under Peale's leadership and increasingly he was in demand for speaking engagements all over the state. The atmosphere throughout the country was light-hearted, gay, and prosperous. These were good times and the bubble just seemed to go higher and higher and get bigger and bigger. That is until one day in October 1929 when the bubble burst. The stock market crashed and the country began to crash. The Great Depression was underway.

Graveyard of Ministers

I wish I had a ten dollar bill for every city across the nation which is supposed to be the "graveyard of ministers." When I went to the Bronx people told me it was the "graveyard of ministers." When I came to Milwaukee people assured me it was the "graveyard of ministers." Naturally when Norman Vincent Peale was considering a call to Marble Collegiate Church in New York City people told him New York was the "graveyard of ministers." The phrase means that if a minister takes a position in a certain town he will soon be forgotten by the rest of the ministry and spend the remainder of his life in that pulpit. In itself, this may not necessarily be a bad thing. Regardless of how long a minister stays in a certain church he should work as if he expected to spend his whole life there. Any town can be a "graveyard" if the minister himself is uncreative or unimaginative and if the congregation is unresponsive and unappreciative of the pastor's labors.

Whether a graveyard for ministers or not, New York must have certainly seemed like a graveyard in general during the early 1930s. In the three years following the stock market crash, the suicide rate for American males rose thirty percent. People were just giving up, jumping out the windows of New York City. The nation was in what economists called the "terminal trough," the most desperate point of the Great Depression. New York was a bleak and emotionally depressed city. Men who had been sitting behind corporate desks were now selling apples on street corners. Jobs didn't exist. There were long lines stretching around the block, not to go to church at Marble, but to wait for bread and soup. Peale recalls, "It was the lowest period economically and psychologically in the United States I have ever seen in my lifetime. Nothing before or since that I have experienced has even remotely approached the depths of discouragement which rested upon the American people, especially in a financial center like New York."

Things had been going well for Peale in Syracuse. He was rapidly establishing a name for himself not only in Syracuse, but around the country. In most Protestant churches ministers are not assigned to a particular post but are invited by a pulpit committee to be their pastor. A "call" is thus extended and the minister has the option of accepting the new challenge or declining to remain in his present church. Peale's reputation had spread around the country. In 1932 he received not one, but two calls to two different churches—one in California and the other in New York City—for the same time.

California was the land of endless possibilities and opportunities. Peale could have been in on the ground floor. And the weather in Southern California in the days before smog was fantastic. Peale was invited to be the pastor of the First Methodist Church of Los Angeles, the largest Methodist congregation in the world.

At the same time he received a call to become the pastor of the Marble Collegiate Church, the oldest congregation in the United States, located on prestigious Fifth Avenue in New York City. It was the pulpit from which men such as Dr. David James Burrell and Dr. Daniel A. Poling had preached for the past forty years. It was also a church in decline. Marble had not had a regular senior pastor for three years. It had become infected with the negativism and depressed spirit which so permeated New York City. Accepting the call to Marble Collegiate Church would also mean that Peale would have to transfer his affiliation from the Methodist Church to the Reformed Church in America.

Peale was ready for a change. He had been at Syracuse for five years; during that time the congregation had grown and he had grown. It was time to launch out in another direction, to take a major step in his career. He knew it was time to change, and he knew that he would go to one of the two churches, but he could not decide between New York and California. Each had points in its favor, and each

A New York street scene

Peale addresses a capacity crowd of 1,250 at Marble.

had points against it.

He prayed, thought, and discussed the matter with his bride of two years, but somehow the answer never came. The indecision went on and got worse. Finally Ruth Peale led her husband into the living room, closed and locked the door, and announced, "We're not leaving this room until we reach a decision!" Husband and wife knelt down beside the sofa and holding hands, prayed for guidance. It was almost two hours before Norman announced, "I think God wants us to go to New York."

"I think so too," his wife agreed. Taking no chances, however, she placed a telephone in his hands to call New York immediately, ending the long period of indecision.

Marble Collegiate Church didn't start with Norman Vincent Peale. It had its origins in 1623 when the Dutch West India Company purchased Manhattan Island from the Manhatoe Indians for $24 worth of beads, colorful cloth, and junk jewelry. The settlement which had begun then had grown to 270 persons by April 1628, when the Dutch West India Company sent a minister to care for the settlers and begin a church. His name was Jonas Michaelius and on April 7, 1628 the first service of the Collegiate Church was held in an empty room above the colony's grist mill. Fifty people turned out for a communion service conducted in Dutch and French. The first church was organized. It was not until 1642 that a church building was actually constructed. Known officially as St. Nicholas Church, it was more frequently called the Church in the Fort. The colony grew and became known as New Amsterdam. Then one morning the Dutch colonists awoke to find the harbor filled with British ships. So New Amsterdam became New York. By

this time there were several churches established and these were known as Collegiate churches because the ministers functioned as colleagues, rotating preaching responsibilities from church to church. In 1696 the Collegiate Church was officially chartered by King William III of England.

In 1854 a new church was built in what was then a cow pasture located at the northern end of Fifth Avenue. At that time Fifth Avenue was nothing more than a dirt road which became a sea of mud every time it rained. The new church was first known as the Fifth Avenue Collegiate Church, later as the Twenty-Ninth Street Church, and finally in 1906 it was renamed Marble Collegiate Church in honor of the solid Hastings-on-Hudson marble of which it was constructed. As New York grew the little farm houses were replaced by brownstones and grand mansions of the very rich. Later these were torn down and replaced by stores and office buildings.

By the time Norman Vincent Peale took over Marble the area had completely changed. There no longer were any residential areas around Marble. It was locked in by commercial and office buildings.

Here was this grand and glorious church, with such a long history, yet it was virtually empty on Sunday mornings. Ruth Peale would sit in the pastor's pew looking at the balconies, supposedly the oldest hanging galleries in the United States, and wonder why they ever put balconies in churches. They looked so forlorn and empty. Two hundred people would come to worship and rattle around in a church which could hold 1,250.

Peale's old anxieties and sense of inadequacy began to surface again. He says, "The old fears that had plagued me from boyhood again ganged up on me. I was now pastor of a famous church on Fifth Avenue and some people were saying that I was too young and inexperienced for so responsible a post— that I just didn't have what it takes . . . (the) problems added up. It was the time of the Great Depression of the 1930s. People were tramping streets looking for jobs which were all but non-existent . . . added to these dismal social and business conditions, the congregation of the church to which I had just come had been reduced to a very small number; and in the large sanctuary, it seemed I was talking to only a dispirited handful . . . The church was really in low spirits and so was I. The old fears grabbed my mind with their icy fingers. Whatever was I going to do? Failure, grim failure stared me in the face! My mind went around in desperate circles, leaving me ever more tense and discouraged and consequently relatively ineffective."

To make matters worse Peale had problems with one of the leading elders of the consistory. The man had an obsession about time and thought the minister should punch a time clock, being in the office exactly at 8:30 A.M. each morning. He would sit during the service, in the boxed off area reserved for elders and deacons, his watch in hand, timing Peale's sermons. At the end of the service he would confront Peale with, "You were two minutes late this morning!" He complained that Peale wasn't spending his time exclusively for the church, and resented the time Peale put into his radio program, writing, and speaking.

After two years of preaching to a small congregation of perhaps 200 persons, Peale was convinced that there was a spiritual depression as well as an economic depression in the land. He was discouraged and depressed. Fortunately the Peales were in a position to be able to afford a European vacation, a luxury not available to most people during the depression. They went to England to visit the little town of Keswick. Peale describes that vacation as one of his greatest spiritual experiences. Sitting in the formal English garden of their hotel, it was time for Ruth Peale to minister to her husband. Peale describes what happened. "As we sat together on that bench that afternoon I again started the dismal recital of my fears. I told Ruth for the thousandth time how discouraging everything was, how tough it was going to be back home what with the depression and bad financial condition. I listed my problems, all of them seemingly so formidable. I expressed my complete assurance of failure.

"Then it happened, one of the top experiences of my life, the beginning of a thrilling adventure in personal change and unexpected but notable victory over fear. My wife Ruth is a gentle, kindly soul but when she gets aroused and becomes firm, brother, she is really firm. Turning to me she said, 'Please stop this negative talk. I've heard enough of it. What are you—a phony? You teach faith—haven't you any yourself? Or are you only a lot of meaningless words? Doesn't God and Jesus Christ mean anything to you?

"'God has given you great potential ability and has called you to unprecedented opportunity for service. You are equal to it if only you will forget yourself. All you think of is yourself—you are involved, tied up, dominated by yourself. And so you walk in gloom and fear until life is hardly worth it. I am so very sorry for you.'

"Then she took my hand in her smaller hand. How soft I always thought it was on moonlight walks, but it wasn't soft now. It had a powerful grip on mine and she said firmly, 'You are going to sit right here with me on this bench until you surrender yourself, and your fears, to Jesus Christ.'

"Then I, who was a pastor, who had been educated to do for others what she was doing for me, meekly asked, 'But how does one surrender? What do I do and say? How can I let go?'

"I can hear her yet speaking out of the native wisdom of the truest heart I've ever known. She said

simply, 'Say, Dear Lord, I now give myself, my life, my mind, my body, my soul to you. I give you all my fears. If you want me to fail I'm willing to accept failure. Whatever you do with me is all right with me. Take all of me. I surrender everything to you.'

"Haltingly I repeated the words after Ruth and in that moment I meant what I was saying, really meant it. That prayer went down deeply into my mind, and came up with the truth, with absolute truth. Suddenly all tension and unhappiness went out of me. I could literally feel it go like a stretched rubber band returning to normal. A sense of happiness—joy is a better word—such as I had never felt in my life surged through my whole being. I had never felt anything like it in my entire experience."

Something happened to Norman Vincent Peale. It was like he had been born again! Indeed, that was precisely what had happened to him. He felt God's healing in his life and he felt God taking away the fear. He says, "Had I not had this extraordinary

The view of 5th Avenue from in front of the Peales' New York apartment. The Metropolitan Museum of Art is on the right, across the street from their home.

experience I'm certain that my life would have been all but ruined by fear, inferiority feelings, and a crippling failure obsession. I realized then that not only I but thousands of similarly beset people could be set free from fear, that terrible destroyer, through the simple formula of surrender. I knew further that this was my mission in life, to explain and urge upon my fellowmen a method of faith and practice literally packed with power, the power to live beyond frustrations and defeats of self and of the world as well."

Peale went back to New York a new man. From that Keswick experience he developed the type of religio-psychological approach which has characterized his ministry. It was just the message that New York City needed! Marble began to change, not overnight, but slowly as the new power in the pastor's life was perceived by the people. The church service loosened up. Peale began using the type of tactics which had worked so well in Brooklyn and

Syracuse. He erected a platform outside his church on 29th Street and Fifth Avenue. Every noon as the office buildings disgorged their workers for lunch, a trumpet was blown. After a crowd gathered a hymn was sung and Peale stepped onto the platform to deliver a short, power-packed message. More and more people began to come to Marble Church. They began to talk to each other in church, even laugh at Peale's funny stories. The word began to spread and more and more people wanted to hear Peale preach.

More and more people began coming into Marble Collegiate Church for counseling. The load became heavier and heavier, the problems more and more complex. One day Ruth Peale asked her husband, "Why not find a good psychiatrist and ask him to work with you?" Peale was introduced to a pyschiatrist, Dr. Smiley Blanton. Blanton was as down-to-earth and direct as Peale and the two hit it off.

The two developed a deep friendship, working together for many years, and eventually collaborating on two books. Together they founded the American Foundation of Religion and Psychiatry located at Marble Collegiate Church. The Foundation gradually expanded and today, known as the Institutes of Religion and Health, it continues ministering to a vast number of people, not only in New York, but all over the nation. It also has a fully accredited advanced training course for ministers, priests, and psychiatric social workers. Its training program is recognized world-wide.

When World War II started, Marble became a magnet for hundreds of strangers and servicemen who found themselves in New York City. Here was a real opportunity to serve and the membership of Marble seized it. They offered programs, a canteen, and Sunday luncheons and dinners for service people. Peale recalls that as much as fifty percent of the congregation in those days would be in uniforms. It was during those days that many people were first introduced to Marble Collegiate Church.

As Peale's prestige grew and he reached out to more people through writing, radio, and television more people also began to fill the sanctuary at Marble Church. Instead of having a church that was empty they now had the opposite problem, a church overflowing with people. Marble Collegiate Church was the first church in the country to install a closed circuit television system to be able to accomodate the overflow crowds.

Marble

It is an unusually warm, sunny, October day in New York City. The sky is blue and the linden trees are shades of russet and gold. It's Sunday morning, and there is virtually no traffic in the city.

At 10:30 A.M. the congregation is already lining up in front of Marble Collegiate Church. The line stretches the entire block from 29th Street along Fifth Avenue and bends around the corner at 30th Street. Ushers walk along the line greeting and welcoming the people and chatting with them. Those in line are well-dressed, a mixture of young and old, but tending to the older. Those in the line appear to be very middle class people. Some have come by subway, others are arriving by bus and taxi, and a few even arrive in long, chauffered limousines.

Emory Ward, an usher at Marble, says, "The crowds—it seems to me that there have always been crowds at Marble, but they've grown over the years, just as Dr. Peale's reputation has grown. I joined the church in 1940 and I've been an usher there for as long as I can remember. Frequently we have to apologize to visitors for the inconvenience that the crowds have caused. I'm always pleased when they reply, 'Wish my church at home had that problem!'"

Most of those lined up in front of the church are visitors. The regular members and the more knowledgeable visitors enter at the 1 West 29th Street entrance. The more elderly members wait in a lounge off the vestibule while the others mill around waiting for the first service, conducted by Peale's associate, Dr. Arthur Caliandro, Marble's Administrative Minister, to conclude.

Carl Cleaver, for many years an elder at Marble, noted, "Sunday after Sunday people gather in Marble Church. They are from everywhere and from every calling, those who have heard Dr. Peale for years and those who have never heard him. They are the fundamentalist and the liberal, the devout and the nonbeliever, the seeker after religion and the mocker, the curious and the indifferent." Marble Collegiate Church today has some members of great wealth and station. There are celebrities. Actress Arlene Dahl with her flaming red hair, looking very much an actress. Art Fleming, known to millions of NBC television viewers as the twelve-year host of "Jeopardy." Julie Nixon Eisenhower was married here, as was one of Charlie's Angels. Both still consider Marble their spiritual home. But there are also tugboat captains and chambermaids, taxi drivers, airline stewardesses, and what seems to be almost a preponderance of businessmen and women. They come from all five boroughs of New York City and from suburban New Jersey and Long Island. Why, you may ask, would anyone drive all the way from New Jersey or Long Island to attend church? Many of these people commute up to two hours every day into New York City to go to work. So why come in on Sunday? Most of the reason can be found in the magnetic personality of Norman Vincent Peale and his messages. In part, it's the friendliness and warmth of a congregation where Christ is at the center and people really share. And in part, it's the sheer thrill of driving into the city on Sunday morning to discover that a ride which usually takes two hours in bumper to bumper traffic, takes only half an hour on Sunday morning!

Most of the tourists who come to see Dr. Peale seem to be white, middle class. But this does not reflect the membership at Marble, for its members come from all races, nationalities, and socio-economic backgrounds.

The 1 West 29th Street lobby is now jammed with people. An usher opens the small, curved, white door which leads into the sanctuary. I find a seat near the front in one of the old pews that fill the main floor of Marble Church. Each pew is in fact a box, numbered, with a door on the end which is shut just before the service begins. This arrangement goes back to the days when pews were rented by individuals or families. One cannot help but feel the

Crowds line up early on Sunday mornings in order to find a seat in Marble Collegiate Church.

history sitting in this beautiful old church with its Tiffany windows and creaking pews and floorboards. The interior of the church has a vaulting, semi-gothic ceiling, the gold arches soaring and meeting in the center. The walls are maroonish-brown decorated with gold fleur-de-lis. A huge pipe organ hangs over the back of the church, surrounded by a U-shaped balcony. There is no pulpit. Dr. Peale doesn't use one, preferring to stand in the center without any obstruction between him and his audience. There is a huge brass lectern with a Bible on top and a brass angel holding a scroll perched on the bottom. The ceiling is covered with television lights and the glare requires getting used to. This service will be televised not only by closed-circuit TV to those who cannot get a seat, but also by cable and satellite TV world-wide.

A well-trained corps of volunteer ushers smoothly guide worshippers to their seats and the church swiftly fills. A young television technician removes a test pattern from the podium. There is a sense of expectancy created in part by the reputation of Dr. Peale but also in part by the television lights, cameras, and technicians. This is the age of the media and the very presence of cameras somehow creates a climate of expectancy and importance.

There are people from all over who've come just to hear Dr. Peale. I overhear the couple behind me introducing themselves as being from St. Louis. Their neighbors in the pew are from Minneapolis. The lady from St. Louis observes, "This is a small church for a man of his stature," and I guess it is.

The head usher says, "You look at your watch and when it's time you get the ministers together and knock on Dr. Peale's door. You go in and he is seated at his desk, generally with his robe on. You know, of course, that he hates to make special announcements, so you try not to give him any but the most urgent. But special requests for prayer, he has to be told about them. Maybe something has just happened, and one of the ministers brings him up to date on that. You keep looking at your watch—it's three minutes to go, two minutes—and you say, 'it's time for prayer.' Here are all these professional pray-ers there, but sometimes it's you who has to say the prayer, everyone standing, all heads bowed. Then you've got to get him out, exactly on the noggen, or else, well, he doesn't criticize, and Mrs. Peale's nice about it, but later she'll intimate that, 'We were a little late last week.'

It's 11:13. Mrs. Peale has been standing talking to someone in that little breezeway that goes up to the choir. She goes out into the sanctuary."

Ruth Peale walks briskly across the front of the sanctuary, down the red carpeted center aisle, to pew number 85, eight rows back on the left side. This is a special pew designated for the minister's family. In the pew is an engraved plaque stating that the Nixons worshipped here while he was President of the United States. Ruth Peale is wearing a light green print silk dress with a kelly green suede coat and matching scarf.

Moments later a thirteen-member professional choir files into the choir loft, followed by Dr. Peale and two associate ministers who take their seats on the huge curved platform. They sit in throne-like, ancient mahogany chairs flanked by an American flag and three huge brass urns filled with yellow and white mums.

The service begins and is very formal, one might say typically Fifth Avenue, New York. The ministers appear to be a somber bunch, sitting, scrutinizing the congregation, frequently not singing the hymns, never smiling. The music is very professional, flawless, and perfect almost to a fault.

I recall a description of Peale given by James Conaway in an otherwise critical article which appeared several years ago in *New York* magazine. It was a classic, and I chuckle as I remember it. He said, "In church, Peale looks over his parishoners like a mother hen, his head resting on folds of black robe." That's Peale! Sitting up there in that huge mahogany chair he looks eighty, and you wonder if he's going to make it through the service.

Peale rises to lead the congregation in prayer. This is a difficult morning for both him and the congregation of Marble Church. They are shocked by the death of Reverend Howard Teusink, a beloved associate pastor of the church, who unexpectedly died of a heart attack the night before. Peale gravely announces the death of his associate and plans for the funeral. Then he begins to pray. When he prays he talks to God. He really does. He talks as if God were standing right there in front of him, and in fact, He is. Dr. Arthur Caliandro, Peale's long-time associate, recalls, "Not long ago I met a man who said he'd been a critic of Dr. Peale. He said that he'd come to church one day just to scoff. 'What happened?' I asked him; I could tell that he was no longer scoffing. 'Did his sermon

The interior of Marble is decorated for Easter with thousands of fresh Easter lilies, flown in from Bermuda by a friend of the church.

reach you?"

" 'No,' he said, 'that didn't get to me, but his prayer did. I felt as if he were praying just for me.' "

It's time for the sermon and Peale explodes to life. The whole atmosphere of the church changes. It loses its stuffy Fifth-Avenueness and takes on a down-home friendliness. It's just like the sign outside the front of the church which promises, "Where Old-Fashioned Friendliness Prevails."

Peale tells how that slogan came about. "Years ago there was a hotel down on lower Fifth Avenue. I forget the name of it, but they advertised Southern cooking, Ohio cooking, Indiana cooking, and whatever. They had a menu card and on it they had these words, 'Where old-fashioned friendliness prevails.' I told the manager on my way out, 'I'm going to steal that slogan and put it in front of my church on Fifth Avenue.' I said, 'You and I are doing business in a very impersonal city. People come here from every small town in America. Let's make them feel at home!' I put that sign in front of our church, it's still there, and old-fashioned friendliness does prevail here at Marble."

Peale starts talking and you forget you're on Fifth Avenue. You might just as well be in a midwest

town somewhere. Peale wears a cordless mike and gestures often while making his point. He avoids the lectern like the plague. His inflection is his own, and he manages to highlight each syllable. He doesn't say "dynamic" but he says "dy-nam-ic." He uses his hands constantly while he's talking. He whispers and then his voice comes on strong. If what he says doesn't convert you the enthusiasm with which he says it certainly will. His sermon this morning is "Enthusiasm Makes Life Exciting" and Peale is certainly enthused and excited about his topic. It's based on an old familiar text to Marbelites, and one of Peale's favorites, the words of Jesus: "I am come that you might have life, and might have it abundantly." It's down-to-earth and understandable. And it's funny! Much of the humor is directed at Peale himself. There are ripples of laughter across the congregation as Peale proceeds to tell a self-deprecating story.

The freshness and humor of Dr. Peale's sermons are recalled by Mrs. Peale in the story of a little boy who came to New York with his parents and attendedf Marble Church. They sat in the balcony where they had a good view of the whole service. She

Peale preaches to his congregation on his 45th anniversary as the pastor of Marble Collegiate Church, while his daughter Elizabeth listens attentively.

says, "Norman was in rare form that morning, and his sermon was full of stories taken from everyday life, some of which had their humorous side. The little boy looked down in wonderment at all the happy faces, then turned to his parents. 'This can't be a church,' he whispered, 'everybody's having fun!' "

Arthur Gordon, Peale biographer, friend, and editorial director of *Guideposts* magazine, says, "To me one of the most remarkable things about Norman Peale is his ability to go on year after year, Sunday after Sunday, preaching sermons that are fresh and fascinating and different. Any traveling lecturer can give the same speech over and over, but every time Norman appears in the pulpit he has to be original—and he is. It would probably take six archangels and six psychiatrists to explain how he does it. I certainly can't."

Emory Ward adds, "Peale tells a message that he makes ever fresh: the power of Jesus Christ to work in ordinary lives. Dr. Peale does not just preach the Bible, he preaches life. And only once that I can recall did I simply not believe what he said to us. That was the day he told us about the man who fell asleep during one of his sermons and started to snore embarrassingly. No one ever fell asleep during a Peale sermon!"

There is the singing of the doxology and a benediction, and the service is over. Associate ministers greet the congregation at the doors and Peale makes a quick exit through the door in the front of the church. Behind this door, down a narrow corridor, is Peale's office at Marble. The long, narrow office at Marble is now used for robing and greeting visitors. The walls are covered with momentos of Peale's long career: awards that have been presented to him, autographed pictures of celebrities and friends. Regardless of how much he would like to, it is just impossible for Peale to stand at the church door and greet each worshipper personally. A few long-time friends and special visitors are received here by Peale. There is the minister who flew in yesterday from Canada just to hear Norman Vincent Peale preach. He tells me, "I've been an admirer of Dr. Peale for many years. I've read all his books. Since Peale is eighty and might not be around in a couple of years I figured I might as well come and hear him." I want to comment, "I wouldn't bet on it!" but decided to keep quiet. A very well-dressed, stylish young couple from Switzerland are shown into the office next, to have their picture taken with Dr. Peale.

Somehow a girl visiting from Buenos Aires who speaks no English finds Peale's office. We learn through a translator that she has been helped and inspired by Peale's books and has gone out of her way to come to New York City just to hear him preach. Mrs. Peale goes out of her way to talk with the young lady, pressing the girl's hand into hers as she does so. Ruth manages to grab her husband and introduce him. When Peale learns that the girl didn't understand a word of his message, he tells her, "It isn't what I said, it's the spirit of what I said. You can understand and feel the spirit even though you didn't understand the words!" Peale is right. The girl is obviously delighted and so is Peale.

Emory Ward says, "Marble's measure of greatness is the millions of people who are reached outside the church. It's the ministry that reaches out with Christian love in dozens of ways, not just on Sundays but every day of the week to every part of the world." Twenty-five percent of Marble's budget goes to outreach through participation in the worldwide mission of the Reformed Church in America, support of that denomination's colleges and seminaries, support of the Federation of Protestant Welfare Agencies in New York City, and support of a number of individual inner-city churches scattered throughout the city.

The spirit of Marble is giving, and it's felt not only in the Sunday morning service, but throughout the week in the various organizations of the church. Each Lent the Marble Single's organization, quite independently from the rest of the congregation, raises ten to fifteen thousand dollars for projects like drug rehabilitation centers, inner-city churches in New York, Missionary Aviation Fellowship, Koinonia Farms, and the like. I know because more than once money from Marble Single's Lenten fund drive came to help my church in the South Bronx. This money is given by young adults—young people in New York paying outlandish rents, with high living expenses, and not always making high salaries. It is money given generously and sacrificially, over and above the normal amount they regularly contribute to the operation of the church.

Each week Marbelites give many hours extending love and friendship in the name of Christ. It may be a tutoring program on the lower East Side, a visitation program to the elderly, making lap robes for people in rest homes, or being a friend and confidant to a troubled youngster. Marble Collegiate Church is a multi-service congregation which reaches out to fulfill the needs of its own members in a variety of ways through a variety of organizations. There is something for everyone. There are single's programs, business and professional luncheons, hobby clubs, etc.

The Institutes of Religion and Health, formerly the American Foundation of Religion and Psychiatry, occupy two entire floors of the adjoining Marble Collegiate Church office building, and offer extensive professional counseling services based on ability to pay. On the staff are psychiatrists, psychologists, and pastoral counselors. In addition the center operates an internship program which helps train pastors in counseling skills, called the Blanton-Peale Graduate Institute.

In 1970 Marble began a program called "Help Line." All over New York City, subway and bus placards appeared inviting people who were troubled, or who just needed to talk to someone, to "Dial-A-Shoulder." Recently the name of the center has been changed to the Norman Vincent Peale Telephone Center. Today a professional staff of seventeen, augmented by over three hundred volunteers deal with over fifty thousand calls each year. A volunteer is on hand twenty-four hours a day to answer calls about personal problems, family problems, health problems. Each volunteer is trained through a fifty-five hour intensive training course before manning the phone. Through this unique

outreach service people's lives are touched and changed, and many suicides have been averted. Volunteers also provide a service called "Cheer-Ring," making over a hundred calls a day to lonely and shut-in people.

To have a minister of international renown like Peale is both a blessing and a challenge to a church like Marble. The blessing is that through Dr. Peale's ministry hundreds are brought into the church. The challenge is for the church not to become simply a preaching station for Dr. Peale, but a real, vital, growing community of believers which will continue after Peale is gone. Peale himself has sought to insure this by building a staff of the best talented and most creative people he can find. To a large extent he has succeeded. In recent years Peale's main function is visibility. His participation in the day-to-day operation of the church is very limited. Yet the church has continued to flourish and develop. The major challenge, however, will come after Peale is gone.

There is no doubt that the church can continue to operate. In order to fully understand Marble Collegiate Church one must also understand something of the history of the Collegiate Church Corporation. Although Marble is the largest and most prestigious church in the Collegiate system, the finances of the Collegiate Church are not controlled by Marble, nor even by Dr. Peale, but by the Board of the Collegiate Church Corporation. The Collegiate Corporation has the unique distinction of being the oldest institution in the new world—three hundred and fifty years old! Its charter was granted by King William III of England in 1696. As such the Collegiate Church Corporation has privileges and prerequisites no one can touch—not the city of New York, the Internal Revenue Service, or the denomination. Through the years, at great legal cost, the Collegiate Church has gone to court to defend the rights and privileges granted to it by King William III. The heart of the Collegiate Church Corporation, as distinguished from the Collegiate Church, is not at Marble, but in an office building at 45 John Street in lower Manhattan, fittingly enough in the financial center. The Collegiate Corporation has several millions of dollars worth of investments and property in the city of New York. I once asked a member of the Collegiate Church Board what the total assets of the Corporation were. He looked shocked and told me flatly that he had no idea. I doubt that even Peale knows what the Collegiate Corporation is worth, or that he could even find out.

Over the years the wealthy members of the Collegiate congregations have donated generous chunks of New York City to the Corporation. King William gave the church most of what is now the Bronx. Wisely they didn't hang onto it! Perhaps the most famous grant to the church was Shoemaker's Meadow. It was given in 1723 by John Harpending and was at that time nothing but rolling farmland beyond the northernmost limits of New York. The Collegiate Church hung onto that real estate. Today Shoemaker's Meadow, still owned by the Collegiate Corporation, stretches between Maiden Lane and Anne Street and Broadway and William Street in lower Manhattan. Here major corporations lease space for their towering, gleaming, glass and steel skyscrapers, bringing thousands of dollars into the Collegiate Corporation coffers.

One of the Collegiate church's most famous edifices, St. Nicholas Church, was located on Fifth Avenue directly across from St. Patrick's Cathedral. St. Nicholas Church was torn down and the land, at Fifth Avenue and 48th Street, is today leased to Rockefeller Center!

Because of intelligent and careful planning, the Collegiate Church continues to give some support to Marble. And three of the Collegiate churches in New York, nothing but shells of what they once were, are now supported, almost totally, by the resources of the Collegiate Corporation. Today thirty cents of every dollar of Marble's budget comes from the endowment of the Collegiate Corporation.

But Dr. Arthur Caliandro and the optimistic staff of Marble are determined that the church is not going to become just another dependent of the Collegiate Church Corporation, but is going to continue its ministry as a vital, living part of the religious life of Manhattan. Caliandro, Peale's heir apparent at Marble, says, "The church is a place which should provide an atmosphere in which a miracle can take place." As long as those miracles keep taking place at Marble it will continue to grow and thrive with or without Norman Vincent Peale. And that's the way he would have it. Peale has always stressed Christian giving and tithing with the result that Marble's congregation raises several hundred thousand dollars annually for current expenses and benevolences.

The sanctuary of Marble is adorned with pine boughs, garlands, and poinsettias for Christmas.

Minister to the World

Questioned about his "self-help books" Peale once protested, "They're not self-help books, they're God-help books!" Peale's writing stemmed from his desire to help people, not just to help themselves, but to find the redeeming and life-changing power of God's love. More than anything else it's Peale's ministry of writing which has made him minister to millions of people around the world. *The Power of Positive Thinking* has been translated into thirty-three languages and over ten million copies have been sold around the world.

It was tough going at first: Peale discovered the great difference between preaching extemporaneously and organizing material into a smooth reading book. More than once he declared, "I may be a preacher, but I'm no writer."

In 1937 Peale published his first book *The Art of Living* which was re-released in 1971 as *The New Art of Living*. In the preface to the original book, Peale made a significant statement of the philosophy behind his writing efforts. "[I believe] that the principles of Jesus Christ contain the secret of the satisfactory life. But ever-increasing masses of the people fail to attend church and so do not come under the influence of its teaching. Moreover, these people feel that the church does not generally talk in the language and thought forms of the common man, with the result that they neither understand nor are greatly interested in giving spiritually oriented living a trial. The Gospel and its power to help everyday people in their everyday lives needs to be restated in simple, current phrases. The workable technique of spiritual power needs to be retaught. The purpose of this book is to give practical help to men and women everywhere in the greatest of all the arts, the art of living."

Peale took his second book *You Can Win* to the same publisher, and it sold only a modest number of copies. After a great deal of labor and frustration Peale finally finished the manuscript of his third book and called it *A Guide to Confident Living*. He decided to seek another publisher and finally settled on Prentice-Hall. This book had much wider acceptance.

After a couple of years he had another manuscript finished, to which he gave the working title *The Power of Faith*. He took it to Prentice-Hall and Peale tells what happened. "The editor said, 'This book won't sell five thousand copies. Why don't you cut it up and publish a book called something like *How to Live 365 Days a Year?* Well, I tried to do that and it didn't gel, so I took the whole manuscript and threw it in the wastebasket. I said, 'This is no good—I'll get rid of this.' I told my wife, 'Someday I'll write another book on a similar subject.' This man slowed me down one solid year with that book. However Mrs. Peale took the book out of the waste can and took it to Prentice-Hall and showed it to Myron Boardman. He decided it was a good book and that's where the title change came in. They changed the title to, *The Power of Positive Thinking*. He worked with me on the book and we finally published it. It started out slowly, but then I was invited to be on one of the early "This Is Your Life" programs with Ralph Edwards. The sales of the book jumped to 300,000 copies immediately as a result of that television program. That gave the book a good start and it went on its way." Eventually the book sold over 700,000 copies in hardcover and millions in paperback.

The publisher was obviously delighted. And the one who had turned the book down? Peale say, "He told me later, 'Well I make mistakes and it was a mistake not to see the potential in the book as you had written it.'"

Prentice-Hall was naturally delighted. Myron Boardman, now Executive Director of the Foundation for Christian Living, was at that time president of the Trade Book Division of Prentice-Hall. He notes, *The Power of Positive Thinking* was not published until 1952, an abnormally long time between successful books, but Dr. Peale had been thrown off stride by an editor of ours who tried to get him to do a different type of book. So Dr. Peale

Peale addresses thousands of people gathered at a "Success Unlimited Rally."

struggled with this, but was not very enthusiastic about it. He has acute instincts about this sort of thing. In time, we were able to convince him that he should go back to his previous approach and give the readers the kind of helpful, direct, reassuring information they were hungry for.

"Somewhere along the line, Dr. Peale had used the phrase, 'The power of positive thinking,' but it wasn't until we got into another one of those title-changing sessions with a couple of hundred titles before us that somehow it hit me and I pulled the phrase out.

"The publishing date was set by the president of Prentice-Hall, Richard Prentice Ettinger, who had a mystical feeling about the number '13.' Prentice-Hall was started on October 13, 1913; the first office building was on 13th Street and Fifth Avenue; it had twelve stories and a penthouse, thirteen in all; counting the hyphen, there were thirteen letters in 'Prentice-Hall.' We all had great faith in the book, but for insurance, Ettinger insisted that it be published on the 13th. We did. October 13, 1952 . . . it was a success immediately. In 1953 and 1954, it was the number one best seller of the year not counting the Bible. Just a tremendous thing. And it made Peale a household word."

Peale's biographer Arthur Gordon points out, "No single factor, clearly, could account for such stunning success. The book had a good title, it was strongly backed by the publisher, it had the prior success of *A Guide to Confident Living* to build on. But beyond all that, and in addition to its spiritual message, it was a peculiarly American book. In it were blended all the idealism and the materialism, the latent religious fervor and the intense practicality of the American people. The book was not afraid to be sentimental, but it was also clear, brisk, and succinct. It pointed to heaven, but it was very much down-to-earth. It had something of the peace of a rural church to it—and something of the pulsing roar of Chicago or Detroit.

"The timing, too, was good. The country was weary and disheartened by the bloody stalemate in Korea. Politically, the long Democratic tenure was drawing to an end. People wanted optimisim, hope, encouragement—a lift. *The Power of Positive Thinking* gave it to them."

Peale's hectic schedule through the years has not allowed him to live the kind of life non-writers associate with a writer: sitting down everyday to a typewriter with few interruptions and completely dedicating oneself to the craft of writing. Peale has tried to use summer vacations for major periods of writing. *Stay Alive All of Your Life* was written during the summer of 1956 in a house in Burgenstock, Switzerland, previously occupied by Audrey Hepburn. Mrs. Peale typed the manuscript as each chapter was written in longhand by her husband. But most books weren't written that way. They were written on scraps of paper during two hour drives between New York City and Pawling, on planes, and in hotel rooms.

Ruth Peale describes how they write: "We have made rough drafts in London and revised them in Madrid and Rome. We have written sections in Holland, Michigan and discarded them in Amsterdam, Holland." Peale told the *New York Times Book Review*, "*The Power of Positive Thinking* was written pretty much everywhere. Because of my schedule, I had to work when I could. Some of it was written in Florida, some of it at my farm in Pawling. There were five solid days on the way to Honolulu, five solid days back. I began in Pasadena—my wife said it was time to stop talking about it and get writing—and one year and one week later we were in the same hotel there when the first copy came. But the material I had assembled over a good many years. It all came out of the laboratory of experience."

Peale had been on the lecture circuit since his days in Syracuse, so his speaking ministry preceded his success in writing. But the success of books like *The Power of Positive Thinking* and *A Guide to Confident Living* put him in great demand. Peale was determined to make his speaking outreach a priority. He had noted the apathy toward religion expressed by many men, businessmen in particular. Yet these men were leaders in the community. He got into conversation once at a banquet with a young business executive on the way up. The man asked Dr. Peale, "What is your formula for living?" Peale gave him a simple, straightforward answer, uncluttered with theological jargon. When he finished, the businessman pointed out to Peale that the church wasn't communicating that message. The message of the church was so cluttered with theological jargon and strange language that the average person didn't understand and as a result was bored and turned off. He challenged Peale, "Why don't you fellows get out of the pulpit and talk to us at our

At a church meeting, Peale fields questions from the audience.

level and in our language at meetings like this? If what you have to offer is worth having, we'll listen. After a while we might even start going to church. But first you've got to play the game on our turf, not yours. If you want us in your churches some of you are going to have to get on the road and sell your product!" Peale determined then and there that if businessmen weren't coming to him, he'd go to them. He decided to become a missionary to businessmen and women. So began the commitment which causes him to crisscross the country each week, living much of his life out of a suitcase, and staying in a different hotel every night.

A major Peale enterprise is *Guideposts* magazine, now the fifteenth largest magazine in the United States. Peale points out that he has more paid subscribers than *Newsweek*. *Guideposts* is "a practical guide to successful living." It carries no advertising, except for *Guideposts* itself, and each thirty-two page issue is packed with personal stories of practical faith as well as testimonies from celebrities. It is a full-color, very slick, very professional magazine. The organization which produces it is just as slick and professional. Peale brags that he has hired away the best minds and talent in the publishing and direct mail industries, from such magazine giants as *Time* and *The Reader's Digest*. He's not just bragging—he has! Because of all the demands on his time Peale's involvement in *Guideposts* must of necessity be limited. To make the magazine successful he has to hire the best people. *Guideposts* is Peale's publishing venture and he and his wife are publishers in more than just name. They are involved in the executive decisions and overall direction of the magazine. *Guideposts* is published not only for the United States, but overseas editions in other languages are geared to different cultures.

The idea that grew into the magazine *Guideposts* came from Raymond Thornberg, a businessman and college friend of Peale's at Ohio Wesleyan. He had the idea for a pamphlet service which would publish stories of people who were living by a strong set of moral values and putting their faith successfully into practice. Thornberg tells how the idea eventuated into *Guideposts* magazine. "Norman had a church with thousands of members, and he was writing books and columns in newspapers and magazines, and he was on the radio every week and later on television as well, and he was getting the American Foundation of Religion and Psychiatry

The Peales' work in their office at the Foundation for Christian Living at Pawling.

under way, and who knows what else he was doing, but when I suggested the idea to him he snapped it up. That day my wife and I were driving Ruth and Norman to an antique shop up on Route 54 near Connecticut so they could buy some furniture for their farmhouse. Right there in the car, Norman, who'd had a feeling for businessmen said, 'If you'll handle the business end of the thing, Pinky, I'll do the editorial.'

"That was the start of *Guideposts*. Today it's the fifteenth largest magazine in the nation. More than that, though, it's helped millions of people in their spiritual journeys, and though it's not a very

money for it. They made time for it, and they worked doggedly."

It was a shoestring operation at best. But it was an operation based on faith. One day a check came in from a total stranger. They gasped! It was a check for a thousand dollars! Mrs. Peale then told her husband, "I wasn't going to tell you this, Norman. But we have a printing bill for $1,059 that I simply didn't know how we were going to pay."

Friends took pity on the fledgling venture and tried to help. Lowell Thomas, a Pawling neighbor, lent them an empty house to use as a publishing headquarters. But on an icy January night the house burned to the ground and took *Guideposts* with it. Everything was gone, including the list of subscribers. The next day Lowell Thomas reported it on his newscast and made a plea for subscribers to send in their names. Another friend, Dewitt Wallace, publisher of *The Reader's Digest*, mentioned the plight of *Guideposts* in his magazine. As a result of the fire, *Guideposts* received so much free publicity that their subscription list doubled! Peale and his *Guideposts* gang began to catch a vision of what the magazine could become. They began to visualize a magazine with one hundred thousand subscribers and began acting as if they already had that magazine, even giving thanks to the Lord, in advance, for the one hundred thousand subscribers. It was a typical Peale approach, and it worked!

Since the beginning of his ministry Peale has used radio as a medium of communicating his message. Radio is essentially a very personal, one-to-one form of communication and it's a medium in which Peale comes across well. The Peales have attempted to use television, but only on public service time. They taped a program in the 50s called *"What's Your Trouble?"* and it ran for eight years. Peale is not a child of the television age, and it seems difficult for him to fully comprehend how to use it to full advantage. He genuinely does not like television and has worked in it only upon pressure. Half-hour video tapes of his message at Marble Church are syndicated across the country on commercial and cable stations for use on public service time and have been enthusiastically received. But he has been unwilling to make his church service a "show" and add the money-raising element used by other preachers in the television media. He believes the gospel should be presented in a dignified and deeply spiritual setting.

publicized fact, for years it's had a vast program of good works. Yet none of these gigantic things would have happened without Norman. He's about the busiest, hardest working man I know, but he can't resist another good idea."

Like many Peale ideas *Guideposts* began around a kitchen table. The table was in the Thornberg home in Pawling. Mrs. Thornberg recalls, "We had a typewriter, somebody else had some pads and paper. For months, it seemed to me, we were writing letters for funds, and I was fixing lunches for the volunteers who came to help. The Peales wouldn't let an idea die just because there wasn't time or

Peale's sermons have always been delivered without notes of any kind. Since they were so helpful, many people wanted copies of them, but there were none available. Back in the 1940s Mrs. Peale began having her husband's sermons recorded. They would be transcribed and she would then edit them and have them printed. People from all over the country began writing and requesting copies, so she organized Sermon Publications with headquarters on her kitchen table. With the success of Peale's books demand for his sermons soared. More than five thousand letters a week were flooding Peale's offices. To handle requests for literature, sermons, and answer every letter became a major undertaking. Sermon Publications was reorganized into the Foundation for Christian Living in Pawling, New York under Ruth Peale's direction.

Today over 125 people are involved in this bustling center of activity. Each month in a publication called *Creative Help for Daily Living,* they mail out nearly 2,000,000 messages by Dr. Peale and others to the fifty states and 130 countries around the world. Over 250,000,000 pieces of spiritual literature have been distributed by the Foundation through the years. There is no fixed charge for any of this material, and the work is supported only by voluntary contributions. Peale's sermons are available in large type for the visually handicapped and on cassettes for the blind. Cassettes of other messages are available at moderate charge. Millions of "FCL" pamphlets have been placed in prisons, nursing homes, hospitals, and military bases.

Each year the Foundation for Christian Living asks its readers to join together in a special twenty-four hour prayer fellowship on Good Friday. Mail bags of requests for prayer from all over the world flood the Pawling office. On Good Friday Dr. and Mrs. Peale join volunteers in the little chapel at the Foundation's headquarters in Pawling to pray in shifts, by name and individually, for each of the thousands of special requests that pour in from all over the world. There are requests for prayer and healing, for restoration of broken relationships, for spiritual and emotional needs, for children on drugs and in prison—they run the whole gamut of human experience.

Both join in prayer in the Foundation's chapel at Pawling, sharing the personal prayer requests mailed in to the Foundation.

Ruth and Norman behind their home in Pawling

Each letter to Dr. Peale receives a response. Mail bags of letters arrive at the Foundation headquarters each day. Each letter is carefully opened and read by a trained staff worker. The materials requested are sent out immediately. Those requesting special advice are sent to a staff of trained counselors who, on behalf of Dr. Peale, write a personal letter giving support, encouragement, and providing the advice requested.

Each morning, when most offices are taking a coffee break, members of the "FCL" staff gather for a prayer break in the chapel. They pray for those who have written in with special prayer requests the day before. The prayer requests are all typed up, the originals go to Dr. Peale and copies on little yellow strips of paper, one or two lines each, are laid on the altar. Staffers go up to the altar, take several prayer requests, and return to their seats to pray silently for people half a world away. And every Friday morning, the entire staff meets in a service of prayer and meditation, at which Dr. Peale, other local ministers, or staff members preside and speak.

Three times a year the Foundation sponsors a "School of Practical Christianity" for pastors and their wives. Heavily subsidized by the Foundation, the four-day seminar costs less than $100 a couple, including meals and lodging! The purpose of these schools is to help those in the ministry apply positive Christian principles to the daily problems of life— the challenge which has occupied Peale throughout his ministry. Pastors have the opportunity of sharing not only with Dr. and Mrs. Peale but with clergy from large and medium-size cities and small rural churches, as well as with other members of the staff of Marble Collegiate Church and with each other. The basic purpose of the school is not how to have a successful church, raise more money or have improved organizational activity, but to deepen the spiritual life of each minister and his wife.

The seminar I attended taught me, among other things, that nobody is perfect—not even Norman Vincent Peale. Early in the seminar it was announced that there was a telegram for me. Later Peale came up and said, "I hope everything's all right." It was kind and thoughtful of him; but his assumption was that a telegram must be bad news. How negative! Actually the telegram was just a message from a member of my church wishing me a good and productive time at the seminar. Well, nobody's perfect.

The Peale Family

Several ladies from Marble Collegiate Church were sitting in the living room of the Peale home at 40 Fifth Avenue sipping tea from tiny china cups when a sharp knock came at the apartment door. Ruth Peale excused herself to answer it and standing at the door was a very irate building superintendent. At this time Margaret Peale was ten, John was eight, and both were supposedly playing quietly in their rooms. A woman walking down Fifth Avenue had been bombarded with a water balloon from their building and a policeman was waiting downstairs. Mrs. Peale, naturally, could not believe her children could have been involved in such a thing. She asked, "Did you see it?"

"No," replied the building superintendent, "but you have to admit that nine times out of ten when I have trouble with children in this building it has started in this apartment."

Later, after the manager and ladies left, the little culprits confessed. It turned out that the target practice from the eighth floor had been going on for some time. The vertical air shaft of the building was littered with experimental bags and balloons which they had used as sand and water bombs. Frequently, these had been dropped on the street. Fortunately, up until now, the children's aim had been bad!

That evening when Dr. Peale came home, John was hiding under the bed. In the parental confrontation which followed, Ruth Peale said, "How could you do such a thing? Don't you realize your father's a minister?" Peale objected, remembering the unrealistic demands placed upon him as the child of a minister.

Margaret Peale Everitt recalls, "Mother was the angry one, but Dad did the spanking."

Mrs. Peale says, "We spoke to the children sternly, telling them that their prank might have hurt someone or caused a lawsuit. We made them go down to the bottom of the air shaft and clean up the debris. We made them pay out of their allowance for

the irate lady's cleaning bill. I forget, now, what other penalties were imposed. But I must confess, one reaction that both Norman and I had, carefully concealed behind our stern parental exteriors, was a feeling of relief and gratitude that our youngsters did have a sense of fun, even if a bit misguided, that they weren't meek and mild goody-goodies, that they were a pair of high-spirited, fun-loving youngsters, even if they were 'preacher's kids.' "

Margaret Peale Everitt remembers another incident. "I called Dad an 'old goat' on the telephone and he was very angry. I was in bed when he came home, pretending to be asleep. He and mother stood there discussing whether or not they should wake me up so they could spank me. I lay very, very still and they didn't. Mother talked him out of it.

"Mother was very controlled. If my kids did what we did, I'd be in a constant rage; but she never raised her voice. The way you could tell that she was angry was that her eyes would glaze and grow large and those pale centers would take on a lot of fiery activity. She was always very reasonable and would speak slowly and calmly."

Peale admits, "Technically speaking, neither my wife Ruth, nor I, qualify as child guidance experts." Yet the Peales have been able to raise three children under hardly normal circumstances, and these children appear to be happy, well-integrated adults contributing to society and raising families of their own. Peale maintains, "A combination of love and discipline is the basic formula." He believes firmly that the cornerstone of their home was faith and trust in Christ, and dependence upon the power of prayer for their family.

I asked Dr. Peale how, with his busy schedule, he found time for his family. He responded, "When the children were growing up we would try and be home for dinner in the evenings as much as we could."

Elizabeth Peale Allen remembers, "The family

In earlier years, the Peales had more time to spend working on their farm in Pawling.

times I seem to recall most were those at dinner. We always had to change our clothes and come to the table. Daddy and John always wore jackets and the girls, dresses. Every night Daddy would tell us stories. There were two of them that he made up as he went along, with to-be-continued installments. One was 'Jake, the Snake,' and the other was, 'Larry, Harry, Perry and Their Magic Airplane.' The magic airplane would land on the back lawn and shrink so that Larry or Harry or Perry could put it in his pocket. I don't remember much about 'Jake, the Snake.' "

As the children grew older, the table conversation veered more to the involvements of the Peales. They tried to draw their children into their work. At that time Peale was writing a very popular column in *Look* magazine and frequently brought home letters selected for discussion around the family table. This enabled him to introduce contemporary moral issues into the talk and get the opinions of his children, as well as sharing his own opinion.

Margaret Peale Everett recalls, "As we grew older, I think Daddy had a genuine desire to know what we thought about things, though there were some subjects that didn't provide much give and take, like drinking and smoking or anything Mother and Daddy were dead against. They had some strong opinions about politics that you couldn't tamper with either. Very strong. Like Roosevelt, for instance.

"I was pretty young when Roosevelt died and I heard about his death in the movies. I had gone to the show with our maid, and they broke into the film and said that FDR had just died; and I said, 'Oh, terrific! Won't Daddy be pleased.' "

"Well, he wasn't pleased, of course, and the maid was simply horrified."

Peale recalls, "We talked about everything. Their interests, their school, what we were doing. 'What do you think about this?' We sought their opinion and they became very involved with us as a result of that. We raised our children as people. We talked to them on a normal basis. They were never kids that were excluded from our thinking."

Somehow their children, like most children, endured and grew through the challenges.

Ruth Peale recalls another incident. "Minister's children, in particular, hear so much about the golden rule and the virtue in 'turning the other cheek,' that quite often they don't know where to draw the line. I remember very well the day John came home from school—he was about seven—and told his father that he no longer liked Roger, one of his classmates.

" 'Why?' asked Norman. 'What did Roger do?'

" 'He said he was going to spit on my tie!'

" 'And did he spit on your tie?'

" 'Yes, he did!'

" 'Did you tell him to stop?'

" 'Yes, but he said he would do it again. And he will, too.'

" 'Well,' said Norman, 'if he does it again, I'd take a punch at him if I were you.'

" 'You would?' asked John incredulously.

" 'Yes, I would!' said Norman forthrightly.

"Sure enough, Roger did spit on John's tie; John did take a punch at him; Roger took the hint and stopped spitting, and the two became the best of friends."

Despite their busy schedules, the Peales always managed to attend special events at their children's schools: basketball games, plays, and Christmas pageants. In spite of all the demands on their time to minister to other people and help other people with their problems, they managed to have time to help their own children with problems. Ruth Peale recalls one night when John was fifteen that he returned home quite late from a party. She was waiting up and they got into a deep conversation over the kitchen table. The conversation got deeper and deeper. Finally, about two in the morning the son decided he was getting in over his mother's head and concluded, "Where's Dad? I ought to be talking with him about these things." In the middle of the night Mrs. Peale roused her husband so he could sit down and spend time having a man-to-man, father-and-son talk.

Elizabeth Peale Allen recalls, "The night before I took my college board exams, I was very tense, very worried. There was such a big buildup to them, and to me my future seemed to hang in the balance. The night before the exams, Mother was away somewhere, and I was unable to sleep. The more I thought about the exams, the wider awake I grew, until finally, I went into Daddy's room. He awakened, got up, and talked with me very tenderly. His words soothed and relaxed me. I went back to bed and to sleep and the next day I took the tests and they turned out fine. I remember thinking that here's a man that thousands of people seek out for their problems and there was I, too, seeking him out in the middle of the night to talk about my sixteen-year-old anxieties. And he didn't fail me."

I mentioned to Peale that these childhoods could hardly be classified as normal. How did he and Mrs. Peale handle these special problems? He answered, "I think this idea that because they happened to be our children they were different isn't true. It didn't seem a problem for any of them except for our son, John. He went to Union Theological Seminary at the time I was getting a lot of criticism from the left-wing clergy. That was a little hard on him because they would talk about me in class right out in front of him. I told him one time, 'John, that doesn't upset me, why should it upset you? Just listen to it and if you can learn something out of it about your father, come and tell me. Don't get upset about it.' He was able to take that and he's a very normal guy."

I am at the Y.M.C.A. conference grounds in Pawling, New York. One hundred and seventy-five ministers and their wives have gathered here from all over the country and from many denominations for the "School of Practical Christianity." Outside, a blizzard is howling and even inside you can feel the cold gusts of wind. Dr. and Mrs. Peale are seated in swivel, molded artificial leather office chairs, sur-rounded by a semicircle of about a couple of hundred people, pastors and their wives. It is a free-for-all session in which we can ask the Peales any questions we want. The questions and answers are frank. "How do you keep from being jealous with all the attention your husband receives from women in the congregation?" "In a busy pastor's schedule how do you find time to be romantically and sexually involved with each other?" The questions go on and on and are fascinating, but the most interesting thing is watching the Peales working together answering the questions. They work like a well-oiled machine. He anticipates what she's going to say, and she anticipates, elaborates, and follows up on what he says. It's like watching a team at work. Peale explains by saying, "Well, that's what comes after living with each other for forty-eight years!"

Both Peales agree that after forty-eight years of marriage they pretty well know each other, have developed a common mind on most things, and don't disagree that much any more.

If there were an irresolvable disagreement? Peale says, "Usually Ruth takes the position that at the long last if I want it that way it's okay. But that's rare—we never get to that point. We resolve it by discussion. But she would, if it came to that."

In-laws created a potentially explosive problem

The Peales in front of their home in Pawling

The Peale family yesterday: (from left to right) Margaret, Elizabeth, John, Ruth, and Norman.

when they were first married. Margaret Peale recalls, "At one point both Daddy's father and Mother's mother lived with us in New York and Pawling. And there were not two more opposite people in the whole world than Charles Peale and Loretta Stafford. Grandpa Peale was a very gregarious, fun-loving man and Grandma Stafford was the epitome of the straight-laced, midwestern minister's wife. She was very sweet. She liked to play hymns on the piano and would get us singing songs like 'The Robin's Return from Florida.' She was also the kind of person who, when you got up from your chair and left the room for a second, would turn off the light and fluff up the pillows. Grandpa Peale was the type to leave his cigar butts smoldering. The two of them disliked each other intensely."

This situation was defused because from the beginning of their marriage the Peales had agreed to be open and honest with each other. Frankly, and privately, they discussed their feelings about each other's parents. Ruth says, "We agreed not to get angry or defensive when the subject of in-laws came up, but to treat it as a kind of good-humored verbal pillow fight . . . and not to do any damage to the fabric of our own marriage." And it worked.

Elizabeth Peale Allen says, "I've never known Mother as anything but even-keeled. But she says

that she was not that way when she and Daddy were first married, though I find this hard to believe. Daddy has always been more volatile; and Mother has intimated that at the very beginning, it was obvious that somebody had to change; and since Daddy was the creative one, it was up to her to try to provide a calm atmosphere in which his creativity could flourish. It was she who changed, very methodically, into a quiet, steadying, supportive force."

"Mother's never been a complainer," says Margaret Peale Everitt. "She's had two very serious ear operations, but didn't burden other people about them. In one of the operations a nerve was struck in some way that a bad metallic taste was left in her mouth; and for months her tongue felt as if pins were pricking it, but she never let you know. On the other hand, if Dad has a cold, you'll know it. But he keeps on. He'll never let anything get him down or in bed. Dad was seventy before he was in the hospital overnight (for a gall bladder operation). Still, Dad is the dramatic one and Mother is just the opposite. John once said that Dad was 'like a cyclone tearing the sky. But at the heart of that cyclone,' he added, 'there is a place of calm.' We all know that the calm of Dad's cyclone is Mother."

Early in their marriage, Mrs. Peale identified her husband's needs and sought to meet them. She realizes that his creativity flourishes best when he is not burdened down with minute and mundane details. Elizabeth Peale Allen says, "Mother has always been Daddy's shock absorber, taking the brunt of things that might bother him, reducing the stress, freeing him for his creativity. She checks in and out of hotels. She's always done the driving (she says it's to give Daddy a rest, but in this case I think she really distrusts his driving). She's always managed the family finances; consequently, he doesn't really know a lot about handling money."

Margaret Peale Everitt says, "Mother is very strong about what she feels a wife's role is, and it's a secondary one to her husband. Yet Mother's many things that the liberation people would like women to be. She's an executive power, a board member, she and her husband share their professional lives. But when they're at home, it's Mother who does the cooking.

"There's nothing that Mother and Daddy do not talk about; they are in constant communication. They are dependent upon each other, but dependent in different ways. Mother's dependence is more difficult to assess. If Daddy weren't making speeches, writing, answering the letters, responding to people, working on *Guideposts* or whatever, then Mother wouldn't have her role either. . . . Her life, she would be proud to tell you, is his life."

But those who think that Ruth Peale is simply Mrs. Norman Vincent Peale had better look again. While she gladly fulfills and enjoys that role in life, she is also very definitely Ruth Stafford Peale. She is the guiding light and organizing genius of many Peale projects, including the Foundation for Christian Living. She has been active in the missionary work of the Reformed Church in America for many years, and because of her keen, analytical mind, sits on many college, and other, boards of directors.

She has her own listing in *Who's Who* which is actually longer than her husband's. She has written her own book, *The Adventure of Being a Wife*, and is almost as much in demand as a speaker as her husband.

Her advice is sought and attended to by her husband; for over the years they have worked together as a team. His ministry is really her ministry. Peale's sermons are delivered extemporaneously and it's Mrs. Peale who sits down with the transcript, edits it and puts what Peale says into readable form.

Peale says, "I'll have to admit it, actually I'm not adverse to doing so, that much of the prosperity I've had and a great big share of the joy of life are because I married right. Marry wrong and—man or woman—you are in for a lot of headaches. Marry right and your life will be full of joy; and prosperity, too."

Elizabeth Peale Allen observes, "When I think of all the problems of other people that Dad has absorbed himself in—and Mother, too, for she's been involved in her share—I sometimes forget that there were times when they had to come to grips with problems in their own family. Looking back, I can see that they met these with the same common sense and effort and prayer that they advised others to use."

Both Norman and Ruth Peale are convinced that after death they will be united with the Lord and reunited with each other. Probably, someday, in heaven, they will be delighted, not only to be in the presence of their Lord, but to be able to keep on together for eternity doing what they seem to do best, touching each other's lives and touching the lives of people.

The Peale family today: Norman and Ruth with their children and grandchildren.

How Do You Do It?

One evening several years ago—Peale was about seventy-seven at the time—I met him after he had just finished speaking to a convention. That day he had traveled halfway across the country and delivered two major speeches. As we were getting into the elevator, I asked him in amazement, "Dr. Peale, how do you do it?" Without any hesitation he replied, "Well for one thing I don't eat the rubbery chicken they serve at these dinners! I just go in late, say what I have to say, and leave."

I have always suspected that Peale's success and enthusiasm in life is due to a lot more. Peale practices what he preaches! He approaches life positively, welcoming each day with the words of the Psalmist, "This is the day which the Lord has made, I will rejoice and be glad in it." He works hard, walks every day, and is as full of vigor and enthusiasm as he ever has been. In the face of the challenges and problems created by his multiple endeavors and the over seven hundred people who work in projects with which he is associated, he maintains a positive mental attitude and sees problems as opportunities.

For instance, Peale has discovered the secret of aging positively. One of his own principles for positive aging is to carefully study persons who are successfully living through old age, and then apply their principles in his own life. Peale says, "Successful old age is built on earlier years lived right." In old age you will be just about the kind of person you are now, only more so. If you are positive and enthusiastic at thirty, you will be that way when you are seventy! If you are a grouch and negative at thirty, imagine what you will be like at seventy! Peale is the way he is now because that's the way he's always been.

He's always believed in pushing himself and working hard. Back in seminary he discovered what psychologist William James called the "first layer of fatigue." That's the point at which most people are tired and call it quits. But James taught that if you can push past the first layer of fatigue, you can develop a second wind and keep on going. The really great people who achieve in life are those who keep on going when the rest call it quits.

In his book *Enthusiasm Makes the Difference,* Peale gives his formula for making any day "good":
"1. *Think a good day.* To make a day good, first see it good in consciousness. Do not allow any mental reservation that it will not be good. Events are largely governed by creative thought, so positive concepts of the day will strongly tend to condition it to be as imaged.

"2. *Thank a good day.* Give thanks in advance for the good day ahead. Thank and affirm the good day. This helps make it so.

"3. *Plan a good day.* Specifically and definitely know what you propose to do with the day. Plan your work and work your plan.

"4. *Put good into the day.* Put bad thoughts, bad attitudes, bad actions into a day and it will take on bad characteristics. Put good thoughts, good attitudes, good actions into a day and they will make the day good.

"5. *Pray a good day.* Begin each day with that powerful affirmation from Psalm 118:24: 'This is the day which the Lord hath made, we will rejoice and be glad in it.' Start the day with prayer and finish it the same way. Then it is bound to be good even if it brings tough experiences.

"6. *Fill the day with enthusiasm.* Give the day all you've got and it will give you all it's got, which will be plenty. Enthusiasm will make a big difference in any day and in any job."

Peale tends to his garden at Pawling.

As Peale goes through each day, he conceives of himself as living in partnership and companionship with Christ. He has a very real sense of Christ's presence in his life and approaches his daily responsibilities with that conviction, but success always has its price. Part of the price which Peale has had to pay for being a preacher, writer, and minister to the world is that he has received more criticism than perhaps any other preacher alive today. Much of the criticism he received came not from the people who were hurting yet were benefiting from his ministry, but from other clergymen. Peale got it from both sides. The fundamentalists accused him of not being a real "born again Christian"; and the liberals accused him of being too fundamental and not following after what was then called the "social gospel." Some of the criticism was legitimate, others were grossly unfair; and some of the criticism came from people who hadn't actually bothered to read what Peale had written. Much of the criticism stemmed from, and became most prevalent following, the publication of *The Power of Positive Thinking*.

I asked Peale how he handled this criticism. He said, "Well, you don't like anybody criticizing you, especially as violently as some people criticized me. I can't say that I enjoyed it, but I decided to take a positive attitude toward it. I decided to listen to it, and if it made some sense to try to get some value out of it. If it didn't make any sense, I determined to try and forget it and never to get mad at those who criticized."

The more popular and successful the book became, the greater the criticism. Some criticized without any real basis from which to do so. Adlai Stevenson is reputed to have said, "I find St. Paul appealing and Norman Peale appalling." Those of his professional colleagues who criticized had more established credentials. Peale recalls one particular incident. "For example, there was a Methodist bishop who was very vicious in his criticism of me, almost hateful. He was a fellow named Bishop Oxnam, and at that time he was the leader of the more liberal wing of the Methodist Church. He wrote a book and I was asked to review this book at the time he was criticizing me the most. I read the book and I was impressed. I thought it was a good book, intelligent, well-written. So I wrote a very favorable review of the book. Finally he wrote me a

letter and said he was surprised that I would write a favorable review of his book. I wrote him back and said, 'Why should you be surprised? The book deserved it!" His assumption was that because he'd been criticizing me, I would write an unfavorable criticism of a book that deserved favorable comment. I said to him, 'I've always tried to be objective.' Do you know that after a while he and I became fairly good friends. He didn't quite stop his criticism, but I guess he saw a side of me that he had never thought of."

The criticism perhaps reached the height of its intensity and greatest personal attack when a national magazine ran a feature in which they interviewed church leaders from across the country who were critical of Peale. Critical is the understatement! They called "Pealeism" a "cult" and stated flatly that it was "blasphemous." Ruth Peale had gotten wind of this article and had actually seen a copy of it well in advance of publication. She recalls, "It seemed to me that the article was not only unfair, but it contained actual misstatements of fact. I told the editors this, but apparently they were less interested in balanced and accurate presentation than in the extra circulation that might result." Ruth Peale, well aware of her husband's strengths and weaknesses, was determined to keep word of the impending article from her husband as long as possible, hoping that somehow it might never appear. She wrote to some of those who had been most critical, pointing out errors on which some of their criticism had been based. But it was too late—the magazine was already in production. The Peales left for vacation abroad but all during their vacation Mrs. Peale was apprehensive about the impending article.

When they got back from vacation not only had the magazine come out, but Peale's father had become seriously ill. It was on the train, enroute to his father's deathbed, that Peale first had the opportunity to read the devastatingly critical article. Some of the most prestigious clergymen in the country were claiming that Peale had discredited the gospel. Peale believed in what he was doing, in his message, and in his methods. The only way out he could see was to resign. On the train he wrote out his resignation as minister of Marble Collegiate Church.

In the midst of this hornet's nest of criticism, Peale's father died. At the funeral his stepmother shared his father's last words with Peale. His father was aware of the intensity of the criticism his son was getting and his last message was, "The Peales never quit! Let Norman know it would break my heart if he ever quit. Tell him for me to tell the others to go to hell!" Peale laughed and cried at the same time and tore up his resignation.

The fundamentalists criticized Peale because he spoke a language they didn't understand. And so they thought he wasn't communicating the same gospel they believed. Peale says, "The reason I got the criticism from them was because I wrote a book that was successful and it wasn't couched in the traditional thought forms and language forms of the church, but in the contemporary language of the day."He continues, "I believe in the Bible as the word of God as sincerely as the most died-in-the-wool fundamentalist, apart from the stilted vocabulary and mechanistic approach some insist upon. I believe that Jesus Christ is the divine Son of God and our Lord and Savior. I believe in the Holy Spirit, I go right down the line with the historic doctrines of the Christian church; but I also believe that this ancient faith can be taught in new and fresh thought and language forms and applied scientifically and with creative power in people's lives, that it can solve the toughest problems of human nature and society, too."

Peale sought to communicate the old, changeless gospel in present day vocabulary and thought forms. To this day he gets criticism from some people who question his orthodoxy because the only thing they've ever read by Peale is *The Power of Positive Thinking*, and in some cases they haven't even read the book, drawing their conclusions only from the title. Peale says, "The book was written for people who didn't go to church. As a matter of fact, the original title of the book was *The Power of Faith*; yet I was never satisfied with that title because I figured it might reach a churchy kind of person, and the one I was really after might be turned off by it. It was Myron Boardman who said, 'Norman, there's a repetitive phrase you've got in this book that you might consider for a title which says the same thing.' He pointed out to me the number of times, unconsciously, I had used the phrase, 'the power of positive thinking.' He said, 'Why don't you call the book that?' He said, "I would think that's synonymous with faith.' I thought so too, so that's what I did. I never started out to write a book on the

power of positive thinking; it just happened to become that."

Peale says, "You will be criticized if there is any force whatsoever to your personality. There is just one way to avoid criticism: never do anything, never amount to anything. Get your head above the crowd and the jealous will notice and attack you. Therefore, welcome criticism as a sign that your life has vitality. Actually, your critic is an asset, though at times an unpleasant one, for he keeps you alert and causes you to study yourself."

If Peale has made any mistake in his long career it has probably been his outspokenness regarding political issues. In 1940 he said, "A minister is a man before he is a minister, and a man or a minister who sees dangerous issues should raise his voice against them." Peale probably would still agree with that statement, although he certainly would choose his issues more carefully. Back in the forties Peale spoke out, understandably, against facism, and in favor of the Allied cause. He also spoke out against Roosevelt and the "New Deal." From the pulpit he criticized labor and management for their respective shortcomings. He spoke out in favor of the nomination of MacArthur on the Republican ticket in 1948 and supported his Pawling neighbor, Thomas Dewey, against Truman. It took a while but gradually Peale began to realize that his public pronouncements and political positions were working against his primary purpose—proclaiming the gospel. In the process Peale had been called all sorts of names, and in many people's minds the emphasis had somehow shifted from Peale's proclamation to Peale's political philosophy.

I asked Peale what advice he would give to young pastors concerning the pastor's role in political issues?

"Aw, stay out of it all together! I wouldn't bother with it at all!"

"But you were an activist early in your career. . . . "

"Yes, but I got over that! I got burned and you wouldn't catch me within a thousand feet of a political candidate."

"Or issues?"

"Not from me! Just stick with the gospel and meet people's needs. Now, if there were some strong moral issues that I thought I should take a position on, I might, and indeed have. But I don't belabor it."

The Positive Principle Today

The definitions given to "positive thinking" are about as diverse as the people giving the definition. Much of the criticism directed against Peale and positive thinking has been from those who have affixed their own definitions to the term, definitions which are not always the same as Dr. Peale's own definition. Peale says, "A positive thinker is a tough, rugged person, who sees every difficulty and faces all facts realistically. But he is not licked by what he sees. He practices the philosophy of optimism which holds that the good in life outbalances the evil thereof, and he believes that in every difficulty there is inherent good which he intends to find."

This is no pollyannish principle which denies the realities of life and life's problems. Dr. Peale is not out of touch with reality; if anything, he is directly in touch with the realities of life. Peale gets hundreds of thousands of letters a year from people all over the world, of all ages and cultures, sharing with him their anxieties, problems, fears, and difficulties. I have had the opportunity to look at some of this correspondence and it runs the gamut of human problems. Over the years, people have come to Dr. Peale, as a pastor and counselor, with every conceivable problem. He has traveled all over the world and seen not only the ghettos of the South Bronx but those of Calcutta as well, observing human misery and poverty. He does not ignore these realities, but he does not choose to focus on them in such a way that they eclipse the rest of life. His feeling is that the way to overcome these difficulties is to focus on the positive and explains, "Don't depreciate life by enumerating all the things that are wrong with it. Things are wrong, and something has to be done about them. But focus mentally upon all that is right about life; life is good, a lot better than not having it, I should think. A lifetime on this earth doesn't last very long, either. It is here today and gone tomorrow. So love it while you can, and be full of enthusiasm."

Now in his eighties, Peale has seen the world go through two World Wars, a depression, Korea, and Viet Nam. I asked him, "Do you think there's a cyclical pattern in our attitudes. For example, the Viet Nam era was a negative time. Negativism seemed to permeate everything; maybe it reached a culmination in Watergate. Now it seems that we're into a more positive era. People seem to be back into feeling good about themselves, about the country."

Peale's response: "I think the pendulum theory is a true one, like Emerson said in his essay on equilization. There is a new attitude. People all over the world are interested in self-improvement. I've been to Australia, Singapore, and have been invited to Belgium next year. And there's a great interest all across our country.

"I've noticed that the audiences in the 'Success Rallies' are primarily made up of young people. I would say that the average age of most of the audience wouldn't be a day over thirty. Hardly any gray heads. Except one. I met an old fellow in Minneapolis. I always try and walk a couple of miles every day, and as I was walking along in Minneapolis a car drew up next to me with a North Dakota license plate. A man and a woman got out and recognized me. The man said, 'Oh, Dr. Peale, I came all the way down here from North Dakota to hear you today.' He told me how far he'd driven, and it was a pretty long drive. He said, 'I came down here because I need to be motivated!' I said, 'That's great!' And he said, 'I'm ninety-one years old!' He came to be motivated! He was about the only old person I saw at any of those rallies, but he was youthful in spirit."

I wondered how Peale views young people today. A few years ago he said, "Some young people seem to have no real happiness in living today. To them, enthusiasm is puerile and outdated. In their search for new values, they experiment in drugs, drinking, sex. But such excesses don't bring about any new healthy values; instead, they send the searchers deeper into the vacuum of nothingness. 'Let's live it up,' they cry, but it sounds like a death watch and there is nothing more tragic than spiritual death in the young. Some who are aware of the deep trouble in the young are shocked and worried. Others condemn them. But all too few look for a creative solution. This is odd, considering that there is a solution both creative and high in potential.

Ruth and Norman walk along the garden path at their home in Pawling.

That solution is simply the application of spiritual enthusiasm that puts genuine honest-to-God excitement back into life."

Today, Peale notices a change in young people and feels that they are showing more "gumption" than they used to. He says, "Many of the young people that I meet impress me a lot. I think they're more back to what they used to be." For awhile Peale had a positive thing against long hair. But he notes, "I don't see so much of that anymore." One thing he doesn't understand about young people is why they wear blue jeans. "I don't see any sense in these blue jeans. I don't think they look good. Now you take a beautiful girl and she wears them, she's dressing down. She isn't showing her beauty off to her best advantage. Why they want to wear ragged blue jeans I don't know. But how they dress really isn't too important—you look at their faces, that's the main thing!"

What does Peale preach about? Positive thinking, right? Partly, but you may be surprised. Allen Broadhurst analyzed 249 Peale sermons delivered between 1946 and 1960 and discovered that the most frequent theme of his sermons—present in ninety-seven percent of them—is the theme of man's relationship with God through Jesus Christ as being the way to happiness and fulfillment in life. Other key themes Broadhurst discovered were: a person's positive mental attitude—positive thinking, present in sixty-five of his sermons; prayer, present in sixty-three percent; faith and its power to solve problems in fifty-eight percent; and the challenge of problems present in fifty-seven percent of his sermons.

Early on in his career Peale sat down and analyzed preaching. He discovered that the great and effective communicators from the pulpit shared five things in common. First, they were arresting. They had the ability to hook the audience's attention at the very beginning through a statement or fascinating illustration. Second, they were logical. Their sermons held together and made a logical progression to the point they wanted to make. Third, they were genuine. They had real honesty, dedication, and sincerity, which could be felt through the message. Fourth, they had a sense of humor. They didn't try to be comedians, but they had a real sense of humor, often self-deprecating, that broke down any tension between them and their audience and helped them to communicate. Fifth, they communicated in simple, everyday, unpretentious language.

Perhaps the highest accolade which can be given to Peale is that he is a skilled communicator, not by virtue of his office as a minister or the fact that he speaks so much, but by the fact that he actually does communicate the good news of Christ. Peale says, "It is my practice before making a speech to any audience to pray for the people present and send out thoughts of love and goodwill toward them." To see him before a speech or sermon you can't help but wonder about that; but when he starts speaking, he virtually explodes. Here is an eighty-year-old man waving his hands, speaking enthusiastically, and exuding energy. It's a transformation which has to be seen to be believed.

Peale has never used notes or a podium. He just stands there and talks. He talks your language, and he talks about your problems, and his problems. Because he has problems too and lets you know it, you identify with him and he doesn't threaten you. The words he uses are down-to-earth words. Occasionally, he throws in some "high-falutin" vocabulary just so you know he has a dictionary too; but that just makes it all the more interesting and down-to-earth. He has a great ability to describe situations, frequently recalling stories from his youth or past experience. When he describes a fire in the fireplace you can hear the snapping of the wood and almost get a whiff of smoke.

Peale has a fantastic sense of humor. He can tell a story unlike anybody else. His timing is always perfect! Frequently the humor is self-deprecating in a good-natured way which makes you identify with him even more. A favorite Peale story—which like most Peale stories should be taken with a grain of salt—tells of a time he saw a man, obviously drunk, weaving his way toward him in a famous restaurant. The man came up to Peale and loud enough for everyone to hear, said, "I can't tell you, Dr. Peale, how much your books have changed my life," whereupon the man passed out on the restaurant floor. Nobody really believes that story, but it cracks them up every time. However, they should believe it, for one night in a southern city, Peale told it, and afterward a man came up to him and said, "You and I are probably the only ones here tonight who know that story is true. I am that man! I was so ashamed of what happened that I vowed I would conquer my drinking problem. I moved to another city; joined the church, don't drink or smoke, and am very active in my church. Thank you, Dr. Peale."

Then there's the mortician convention story. Whenever he tells it, the story always begins, "The other evening I happened to be in Indiana speaking at the National Morticians Convention. . . ." One would think he spoke every other day to undertakers! The story goes that Peale showed up in a tuxedo and everyone sitting at the head table was to wear a white boutonniere. A woman undertaker had the privilege of affixing Peale's flower. She fumbled around, unable to get it on correctly and in the process stabbing both herself and Dr. Peale. Finally in desperation she said to Peale, "You know, I could do this better if you were lying down!" It never fails to bring down the house. And every time Mrs. Peale hears it, and she must have heard it a million times by now, she manages to laugh at all the right times just as if she never heard the story before in her life!

Dr. Arthur Caliandro says, "About five years ago I started asking Dr. Peale if we couldn't get together and talk about preaching. I wanted first hand advice from the greatest communicator in the country. 'Sure,' he'd say, 'we'll do it sometime.' But we didn't, and when I finally pinned him down to a time, he was vague and changed the subject. Naturally, I'd been studying him carefully for as long as I can remember. I knew that everything he read, everyone he talked to was potential Sunday material. I knew that he mapped out his sermon all week, at home, in airports and hotel rooms, in spare moments; that he pulled it all together on Saturday, and that he always worked five sermons ahead. But I didn't know the how of his preaching, and he wouldn't tell me.

"One day I asked Mrs. Peale, 'Why can't he help me?'

" 'Because he doesn't know how he does what he does,' she said.

"Which, I guess, is the way it is. Still, I've continued to look for clues. One of them Mrs. Peale herself gave me when she said, 'Norman stays steeped in people's problems.' It's true; he's always with somebody else in his thinking. You can tell it even when he's away from the church by all the letters he writes, longhand, to members of the congregation and all the telephone calls, often to people he doesn't know, like somebody's aunt in San Antonio who's in distress.

"And another clue is: he's a lover. Sitting up there beside him Sunday after Sunday, I can see—no I can feel—the love that goes out to the people in

Peale signs autographs following a "Success Unlimited Rally" speech.

front of him."

Peale's sermons, according to Caliandro, are geared to giving answers, providing workable steps for the listener to use to implement his goals, to giving hope, and to bringing the people to a commitment to Christ. Caliandro says, "Peale preaches consistently good and relevant sermons every Sunday." Peale has sometimes been criticized by other ministers for using too many stories and illustrations, but Caliandro points out that Peale is only following the style and method of the master storyteller of all time, Jesus Christ. Christ always used stories and illustrations to make his point.

Peale explains his preaching with a story. "You have heard the old saw about the minister who explained how he planned a sermon, 'First I tell what I'm going to talk about, then I talk about it, and I tell them what I've talked about.' That's pretty much what I do."

The Greatest Positive Thinker

Norman Vincent Peale has offices scattered all over the place and scarcely uses any of them! Most of his work is done on the go. He never travels without a briefcase bulging with work to be done enroute.

Once, when his children were young, Peale was rushing out the door, without his briefcase. His daughter Elizabeth ran after him yelling, "Wait, Daddy! You forgot your brains!" Ever since, Peale's pile of traveling paperwork has been called "Daddy's brains."

Peale has offices at *Guideposts* Associates in Carmel, and in New York City; offices at the Foundation for Christian Living in Pawling, New York; and an office at Marble Collegiate Church in New York City. His working office is located in a professional apartment, the type used in New York by doctors and dentists, on the first floor of an apartment building at 1025 Fifth Avenue, directly across the street from the Metropolitan Museum of Art. The building has a side entrance on East 84th Street, making it conveniently located right across the street from Peale's New York apartment.

When I went to see him recently, a uniformed doorman, not uncommon in New York apartment buildings, was expecting me and escorted me to Peale's suite of offices. From the outside the door looks like any other but recessed in the combination doorbell-peephole is a faded name tag, "Norman Vincent Peale." The doorman rings the bell and we wait. We try again. There is no answer. It is Sunday afternoon so there are no secretaries in the office. The doorman assures me that I am expected and tells me to wait while he goes to the front and buzzes Dr. Peale on the intercom. I wait, and a little while later I can hear the intercom buzzing inside. I hear someone walking around and muttering. Finally the door opens and Dr. Peale invites me in. "I'm sorry I didn't hear the door," he says, "They've been buzzing me on this thing but I don't know what to do about it. I'm not here enough to know how the thing

works." He throws his hands in the air.

Peale's hands are expressive and he often talks with his hands. A longtime friend of his who was watching me photograph him said, "Be sure to get his hands! He always talks with his hands!"

The suite of offices is deserted except for Dr. Peale. It's rather stark, almost bleak, with standard New York landlord-issued white walls. There are four wooden desks, bulging files, and electric typewriters; the only touch of luxury is a plush, Persian carpet in the entry. An old-fashioned glass door bookshelf is filled with his books and, on the top are various awards he's received, including medals from the Freedoms Foundation at Valley Forge and his Horatio Alger Award. Hanging on the wall of the improvised lobby is a Bachrach portrait of Peale in full academic regalia.

Peale's own office is the same stark, standard-issue, white; the carpet is gray and so are the curtains. The mahogany desk is small, efficient, certainly not designed to make any kind of statement of power or prestige; and there are several chairs, lamps, and a green and yellow striped sofa. One wall is lined with bookshelves. On the other wall are pictures of the Peale family, framed enlargements of photos which appeared in a magazine article about Peale. They are candid, informal shots of a relaxed and happy family. In one of them Peale is sitting on the edge of the bed, tweaking the nose of daughter Elizabeth, who's in bed with a cold. There's a framed composite picture of his children's wedding pictures; and above the desk, a large picture of Ruth.

And on the floor is another Oriental rug, again the only hint of luxury. The Peales like Oriental rugs and seem to use them wherever they have an excuse to do so. In one of his books Peale pokes fun at his wife's expensive taste in rugs; but since genuine Oriental rugs have turned out to be one of the best investments possible, I doubt that he pokes fun at her taste any longer.

Reverend Norman Vincent Peale today

A multi-line telephone sits on his desk, the handset of the phone has a sterling silver cover engraved with "Norman Vincent Peale" and decorated with a gold Mack bulldog, which was the gift of Zenon Hanson, former president of Mack Trucks, whose symbol is the bulldog. The telephone system interchanges between the office and the Peale home across the street so he can buzz his wife on the phone intercom. Indeed she buzzes us during our conversation to check on him.

These offices are the nerve center of Peale's vast interlocking ministries; and yet he is so busy, so constantly on the go, that he seldom has time to even use this office. And most of his work must be done in airplanes and hotel rooms around the world.

Peale gives no thought of ever retiring. "The question with me," he says, "is what would I retire from? Would I retire from the speaking business which is a large part of my activity? Would I retire from *Guideposts* magazine? Would I retire from the church? There is no way I could ever retire and be a gentleman farmer! The minute I'd leave one job I'd have another to do, and there's no way I could retire from them all!"

Does Peale, now in his eighties, ever think of death? I asked him this the day after a close and trusted associate minister of Marble Collegiate Church had suddenly died of a heart attack. "When a friend dies so suddenly like last night it makes you think about it. But I don't go around thinking about dying. I just go on and live my life."

I asked if it were possible to apply the principles of positive thinking to death and view it as an opportunity. "Yes, I've always taken that attitude. I believe that if your life is in Christ, if you're a committed Christian, and if you've given your life to Christ, that death is not the end. It leads to something greater! You will live beyond the grave and be with the Lord and continue to live constructively in an even greater kind of life. I have no doubt about it, based on the promises of the Bible and what I know about God and Christ, that you will live beyond the grave, you'll see your loved ones, know them, and have relationships with them."

While he doesn't brood about death, Peale's faith enables him to look at it realistically and positively. A favorite illustration of his—and mine —is about death and he frequently uses it at funerals.

"Before you came into the world you were an unborn baby. We all were. As we contemplate going

Peale baptizes his grandson, Andrew Allen, the son of Elizabeth and John Allen.

from this world into another, we are again unborn babies so far as that other world is concerned.

"Now if a baby not yet born, still tucked under his mother's heart, could think, he might say to himself, 'This is a wonderful place. It is warm. I'm fed, I'm taken care of, I'm secure. This is a great world where I now am. I like it.' And then someone might say to him, 'But you're not going to stay here. You have to move on. You're going to die out of this place. You're going into another world.' That baby would look upon the process of birth as if it were death, since it would be the end of the pleasant state he was in. And he would protest, 'I don't want to die. I understand it here and feel secure. I want to stay.' What to us is birth, to him is death, and he resists it. But the day comes when he does die to that life and is born into our world.

"What happens to him? He is cradled in loving arms. Soft hands hold him gently. A kind face looks down at him, and he loves that face. Everybody that comes near loves him. He is the king of the world he surveys. Then he begins to grow, and he finds life good. He has some struggles and hardships, of course, but that is to make a man out of him. He has difficulties and sorrows, but he loves God and

people love him. And he loves this world, with its seasons, its beauty, its human companionship.

"Finally, he gets to be an old man and is told, 'You have to die.' He protests, 'I don't want to die. I love this world. I like to feel the sun on my face, and the cool rain. I like our dear, human ways. I love the faces of my wife and children. I've lived here a long time. I don't want to die.' But he does die to this world and is born into the next."

Peale concludes this illustration with the challenge, "Now can you believe that all of a sudden the character of God and the constitution of the universe are going to be changed so that a person will be born into a forbidding place of gloom or terror, or will be left in a state of nothingness? That is preposterous!

"He will awaken to find himself young again. Loving faces will greet him; loving hands will touch him. More beautiful sunlight will surround him; sweeter music will sound in his ears. All tears will be wiped from his eyes, and he will say, 'Why was I so afraid of this thing called death, when, as I now know, it is life?' "

Peale remembers making his own peace with death while still a small boy, standing beside his grandmother's grave in a little country cemetery in

Ohio. The minister read the words of Jesus, "I am the resurrection and the life; he who believes in me, though he die, yet shall he live, and whoever lives and believes in me shall never die." (John 11:25-26). Peale remembers, "I was just a boy, but suddenly my eyes were blinded by tears and a strange warmth filled my heart. It was one of those deep spiritual moments when certainty comes into the human mind without argument, without demonstration, without experiment, without tangible proof. I knew the words I had heard were literally, finally true."

Peale sees death not as a dark door, or forbidding valley, but as a bridge stretching between two marvelous worlds. There is nothing to fear for the one who has a positive, living faith in a good and loving God.

Peale tells of a time when he and Ruth were flying from Honolulu to New York. He had fallen asleep and awakened just as the plane met the dawn over the western coast of the United States. He looked out the window and saw Mt. Shasta rising out of the pink morning mists that clung to the earth, high above all other mountains. "The sun was bombarding its eastern face, turning it into gold and pink and all the bright colors of the morning. It stood resplendent in all its glory, pushing its great cone up above all the darkness that was around it. As it stood above all the mists, above the surrounding mountains, it was an unforgettable sight . . . I sat there thinking that eternity must be something like that. We move up above the clouds and darkness into a higher level of life, to a place of cleanness, light, and sunlit beauty. So it shall ever be to the person who has a deep and positive faith."

As a pastor Peale has had to deal with death all his life. It has not always been easy. He recalls, "I shall never forget the second funeral I had to conduct as a young minister. A little girl had died. She was about eight years old. I can still remember her, lying in her casket as if asleep, with pink ribbons in her hair. The young parents sat nearby, stunned with grief. I was so young and inexperienced myself that I seriously doubted my ability to conduct the service without breaking down. So before it began, I did the only thing I could think of. I went over and sat between the father and the mother and put my arms around them and told them, through the tightness in my throat, that I loved them. Later, the mother told me that this gesture touched and helped her more than anything I could have said or done."

Peale faced the grim realities of war and death on a nondescript pile of red earth with the name of Hill 55 in Vietnam. He was in Vietnam at the personal request of the President. An improvised altar and public address system had been hastily set up, surrounded by sandbag bunkers. Seated on the ground were seven hundred young men of the Seventh Marine Regiment, all dressed in combat gear with rifles by their sides. In front of Peale, as a grim reminder of the heavy casualties this unit had already suffered, was an M-16 rifle, upside down, bayonet thrust into the red earth, with a helmet hanging on top. Peale could look out and see the hills in the distance where the Vietcong were encamped. Heavy fighting was ahead, and it was likely that many, if not most, of these young men would not live to see their homes and loved ones again. A military band played as the soldiers sang some old hymns. Then Peale stepped to the microphone dressed in the olive drab fatigues he wore in Vietnam. Stenciled above one jacket pocket was the word "Pastor" and above the other, "Rev. Peale." It was probably the most difficult preaching assignment Peale has ever had. There was a grim hush and except for Peale's voice, no sound except the explosions of shelling across the river.

Peale closed his talk with these words. "In the solemnity of this moment, we must face the fact that you are the ones who are called upon to endure the stress of battle. You are the ones who must bear the heat and the burden of the day. May the good God, your heavenly Father, and your Savior Jesus Christ watch over you and protect you and keep you from harm. But if, in the uncertainties of battle, the moment comes when you, too, are called to go forward with your fallen comrades, may you meet it bravely, and know that your soul is clean at the last, and that another life is just beginning. And may we who are older and cannot fight the battles everlastingly keep faith with you, so that together we shall turn not only our own beloved country but the whole world into a place of peace and goodwill.

"As for those who have died here, we can say about them the greatest thing that can be said about any mortal man: 'Greater love hath no man than this, that he lay down his life for his friends.'"

Peale sat down and there was profound silence, except for shells exploding in the distance. A Marine stood up and sang "How Great Thou Art" and a bugler played "Taps." Peale boarded his helicopter and as it rose into the air he stepped to the open bay and below him saw the Seventh Marines, standing at attention on Hill 55 saluting him, Norman Vincent Peale. He waved his hands and the ranks broke as seven hundred enthusiastic young men, many of whom, as it turned out, died in the weeks of fighting that followed, stood waving and cheering. As the helicopter rose, and two others moved in to protect Dr. Peale, here as a personal representative of the President, Peale collapsed in his seat and cried unashamedly. It was a long way from Fifth Avenue.

I asked Peale what would happen to his ministries when he was gone. "We've never gone into that. I think they will go on. *Guideposts* magazine will certainly go on. The Foundation for Christian Living will go on. They've got a great backlog of unpublished material that I've written that they can use for years to come, and we are regularly sending articles by other ministers and inspirational writers. The church would naturally go on." Reluctantly almost he admits, "The speeches that I make to all kinds of business conventions wouldn't go on, but the rest would!"

Peale loves life! He says, "Cultivate the ability to love living. Love people, love the sky under which you live, love beauty, love God. The person who becomes enthusiastic is filled with the sparkle and the joy of life. And then he goes on to fill [life] full of meaning." Peale is enthusiastic about life! He says, "I have known people who remained enthusiastic until the end of their lives and then seemed to go out of this world with flags flying, the light of enthusiasm for life still in their eyes."

When Norman Vincent Peale leaves this life, as undoubtedly he must, if he has his way, he will go with flags flying and filled with enthusiasm. More than anything else Peale fears the disease called "psychosclerosis" a "medical" term he coined to describe hardening of the psyche, and a loss of the love and enthusiasm for living. For Peale, enthusiasm is a young trait which belongs to those who are young in heart and spirit, regardless of their chronological age. Peale may be in his eighties but he is young and enthusiastic in spirit and vitally involved in living.

I asked Peale if, when he preached his first

Peale prays with the Marines on Hill 55.

sermon, ever in his wildest imagination he conceived that it might be possible for one man to have the positive impact which he has had on the world. He replied, "No! Nothing like that ever entered my mind. I was just excited by life, it was opening up, and every new experience was an event." He continues, "A long time ago I developed what might be called an obsession to try to help people get the best from life, and learn how to live with its hard experiences in a creative manner." Peale believes that this can be accomplished through the positive message of Christianity. He says, "We must capture the world with Christianity. We must make the church bigger until all the people are in the church ... Jesus Christ wants everybody ... He tells us to go into the highways and byways and bring them all in."

Peale's greatest satisfaction in life has not come from all the awards and accolades he's received, nor from the honorary degrees conferred upon him in abundance, nor from his twenty-two books, or his record of selling over ten million copies of one book, nor from any wealth, power, and prestige that have come his way, and not even from his loving relation-

Peale speaks to the congregation of Marble.

ship with his wife and his family. He says, "My chief satisfaction has been getting people to accept Christ and order their lives on that level."

Back in 1955 Peale was invited to preach at a newly established congregation of the Reformed Church in America in Orange County, California. It was a congregation being started by a young minister from Iowa by the name of Robert Schuller. Of course nobody had ever heard of Robert Schuller then. It was an unusual beginning for a church because Schuller was conducting his Sunday morning services in the open air setting of the Orange County Drive-In Theater. Schuller had taken out a large ad announcing that Norman Vincent Peale would speak and the drive-in was packed with cars. A podium of sorts had been erected on top of the drive-in's snack bar. Peale sat there on a metal folding chair with young Robert Schuller waiting for the service to begin. Schuller told him enthusiastically about the great church that this would someday become. Peale says, "I knew then that it would be in fact, for it already existed in his mind, and he had the energy, ingenuity and the faith to bring it to pass." The hot breeze whipped across the tops of the parked cars making the tar top of the snack bar sticky.

Robert Schuller stood up and looked out over the combined glare of the sun reflecting off the windshields of over a thousand cars. Enthusiastically he began to introduce Dr. Peale. He said, "Our special guest this morning is one who needs no introduction. His name is a household word. He is known and considered a friend by people around the world. His inspired sayings have helped millions of people. He has touched and transformed lives and helped people believe in themselves and achieve their possibilities." Peale began to squirm in his seat. But Schuller continued, enthusiastically, and dramatically, "He is in fact the greatest positive thinker in the world. . . ." By now Peale was blushing. Then Schuller announced with a triumphant flourish, "His name is Jesus Christ! And here to tell us about him is Norman Vincent Peale."

No introduction could have pleased Peale more! For this is just what he has been doing now for almost sixty years. I asked him what he would like to accomplish yet in his lifetime. He said, "I have no new goals; it's an old goal. In fact it's the same goal I've been working on since I started; and that's to reach as many people as possible and persuade them to be followers of Jesus Christ. Jesus has the answers for them, and for the world."